TANSY

CW01509239

Ten
Drink
Less
and
Live
Well

Find Freedom from Overdrinking:
A Complete Guide to Lasting Change

Synergy Publishing
Newberry, FL 32669
publishwithsynergy.com

Ten Steps to Drink Less and Live Well
Find Freedom from Overdrinking: A Complete Guide to Lasting Change
By Tansy Forrest

This edition first published 2025.

International Standard Book Number: 978-0912106434

International Standard Book Number eBook: 979-8-8815-0644-5

Author: Tansy Forrest www.tansyforrest.com

Literary Agent: Wendy Yorke www.wendyyorke.com

Designer: Cris Convery hello@crisconvery.com

Editor: Nicole Howes hello@thebracket.co.uk

Disclaimer:
The information provided in this book is for general informational purposes only and is not intended as, nor should it be considered a substitute for, professional medical advice, diagnosis, or treatment. Always seek the advice of your physician or other qualified healthcare provider with any questions you may have regarding a medical condition. Never disregard professional medical advice or delay in seeking it because of something you have read from this book.

MIX
Paper | Supporting
responsible forestry
FSC® C163799

Dedications

To everyone who experiences challenges when dealing
with alcohol.

I wish you strength and courage on your journey.

Acknowledgements

My husband Tom; for his patience while I wrote my first book. My Mum and Dad; for encouragement throughout the project.

My beta readers; for their fantastic support and insight.

All those clients; who have permitted me to use some of their experiences in anonymous case studies throughout the book. Thank you for sharing and helping others. I have learnt so much from you and it is my honour to have worked with you all.

Piotr Sznicer; my great therapist, who helped me to live a more balanced and happier life.

Wendy Yorke, my author coach, editor and literary agent; whose faith in and appreciation of my work was instrumental in making this book happen.

Synergy, my publisher, for believing in this book and supporting it every step of the way. Your guidance and expertise have meant so much.

Thank you all!

Praise For This Book

"Wow, I absolutely love this book! It's easy going, approachable, and entirely and immediately applicable no matter where you are on your moderation journey! It came at a great time for me because I had just wrapped up a particularly difficult year of trauma history and heavier drinking due to personal issues, with many alcohol overindulgences. However, I learned from my lapses using your method and am being successful again in 2024 on my moderation journey. I will recommend Tansy's book to my colleagues because the exercises are wonderful and can be used for clients, as well as oneself."

Anonymous client, California, United States of America

"As a doctor who has specialised in treating alcohol use disorder using The Sinclair Method for the last seven years, I was delighted to meet Tansy, learn of her own journey, and I have been privileged to read her book. Tansy delivers a heartfelt message grounded by her personal experiences of adversity and also her extensive professional experience of helping others. *Ten Steps to Drink Less and Live Well* is an essential text for anyone intending to have a more healthy relationship with alcohol, manage anxiety, and provides a framework to manage stress. I will be recommending this text to all my patients who are struggling with stress, anxiety, difficulty navigating adversity and addiction."

Dr Janey Merron, National Health Service general practitioner, private general practitioner and Chair Medical Advisory Council, Nuffield North Staffordshire Hospital, designated doctor Child Safeguarding North Staffordshire and Stoke-on-

"This is without a doubt one of the most complete books you can read about a subject that is very hard to handle. Every aspect of coping with the complexity of non life-threatening alcohol use disorder is handled in this book in a practical way. The reader can clearly decide if the methods in this book are suitable for them. A great deal of useful information is presented as a means to reach a stable way of living with moderate alcohol use."

"What I liked most was the fact that the structure was very logical. Questions that came to my mind during reading were all answered in the sections after that. Tansy's book stays to the point and doesn't get boring for one moment. I enjoyed it from beginning to end. I also like that every aspect of moderation has been included and I know I will use it in the future, not only as a way to moderation, but also to maintain moderation, which is treated thoroughly. I am already talking about this book to my friends and family because of the successful treatment that I experienced and I highly recommend it."

"This book is a great read. It is written with kindness because it is such a private issue, and not being judgmental or aggressive in suggested behavioural changes is helpful for so many people. I think Tansy's approach for someone who is worried about their drinking is supportive and most importantly, progressive in advice. Her content is well researched and backed up with proven, practical methods, together with strong case studies and genuine, constructive goal-related strategies. I will definitely direct clients to you. Congratulations."

Georgia Foster, clinical hypnotherapist, author of *Drink Less In 7 Days*, Australia

"Tansy's book presents a wonderfully holistic approach to taking charge of your relationship with alcohol. I am really happy to feel like I am in control of my drinking again after working with Tansy and her book has given me the confidence to believe I can make other positive changes in my life. I think it has a wonderfully approachable writing style, which comes across as very knowledgeable and compassionate. It was also really interesting hearing more about the author's personal story and exploring The Sinclair Method. If anyone talks to me about needing help to cut down their drinking, I will recommend this book first. Mostly because it is approachable and I had a very good experience using this method."

Anonymous client, United Kingdom

"Tansy's book is an easy to follow guide to cut down on alcohol. It is informative regarding dealing with lapses, relapses, triggers, and how alcohol use can affect an individual. Many of my clients mention to me how they would like to reduce their drinking, but they find it difficult to cut down when they are around certain friends - this book clearly deals with these topics. I really liked how Tansy stated her alcohol issue and the approach she used for moderation. She has both personal and professional

understanding of the subject. The case studies in the book show you that you are not alone and you can also reduce your alcohol intake, as other people have done successfully. I will recommend this book to my clients, family, and friends."
Valerie Davis, hypnotherapist, United Kingdom

"I enjoyed this book's kind and encouraging tone and comforting approach. Good personal stories - can never have too many. I love Tansy's concept of a 'Moderation Journey' and how to put it into practice, which is so much kinder than an all-or-nothing principle. Yes, I will certainly recommend this compassionate book to my friends, family, colleagues and clients."
Sarah Peacock, estate agent, France

"This was an amazing read. It is relevant, on topic and flows very well from chapter to chapter.

I appreciate how – from the very beginning, the journey to alcohol moderation is viewed as an enjoyable experience, which was a unique and whole new approach for me. With my alcohol use, I was very depressed and desperate for the answers, solutions and changes."

"I will recommend this book to my clients, colleagues, friends and family because of its unique and compelling narrative and because it provides the complete package. Readers benefit from the abundant knowledge of the written content; the supportive recordings; and the incredible worksheets, exercises and journal prompts to actively monitor and track personal progress. I have not seen a self help book written before with such a well-rounded coverage of its topic. In my line of work, often clients are dual diagnosis so offering the information in different learning styles is another reason why I will highly recommend this book to my clients who are struggling."

"Alcohol was always my master but after reading this book I am now the master of alcohol."

Jacinta Smith, National Disability Insurance Scheme support worker, Australia

"I really enjoyed reading Tansy's book! My favourite parts were the real case studies of how everyone navigated the moderation journey in their own way. It feels so creative and unique to everyone's journey, and made me feel more connected to like-minded groups. It was an easy read, which I appreciate having a busy life, and I love the compassionate approach."

Anonymous client and therapist, The Netherlands

"*Ten Steps to Drink Less and Live Well* is the perfect companion for anyone looking to improve their relationship with alcohol. Tansy's insights, alcohol moderation techniques and hypnotherapy recordings have given me the belief to make positive changes in my life. I enjoyed it most because it emphasises our own power to make changes is within our control. This was reinforced by the case studies and real-life client stories. Also, the worksheets provide the tools to build your own plan, with Tansy guiding you through it. Her moderation and hypnotherapy combination make the book unique and special. I will certainly recommend her book to friends or family members who want to cut down on their drinking."

Anonymous client, UK

About The Author

Tansy Forrest
Dhyp, MNCH, BA (Hons), PGCE, MA

I'm Tansy Forrest, a clinical hypnotherapist based in South London, UK. I specialise in helping people with alcohol moderation and cessation, weight loss, and sleep issues. Before becoming a hypnotherapist, I worked in education, teaching Social Sciences and rising to Head of Department. I also completed an MA, focussing my research on individual and group motivation.

Despite my professional success, I struggled with stress, anxiety, and the pressure of balancing a demanding career with personal responsibilities. Panic attacks, constant worry, and unhealthy coping mechanisms left me feeling trapped—until I discovered hypnotherapy. It completely transformed the way I saw myself, helping me break free from negative patterns and regain control of my life.

That experience inspired me to retrain as a therapist and help others do the same. My approach is progressive, focused not just on the past but on retraining the mind for a better future. I truly believe that everyone has the power to change, and I'm passionate about guiding people toward emotional wellbeing and lasting transformation.

Is This Book For You?

This book is for you if you experience problems in relation to drinking alcohol, either through binge drinking, or daily habitual drinking, and you want to cut down to safer levels.

This book is not for those who are physically addicted to alcohol.

How You Will Benefit From Reading This Book

The main benefit of reading *Ten Steps to Drink Less and Live Well* will be to discover and enjoy a newfound ability to cut down on alcohol painlessly, and to really enjoy the journey. This will improve your: health, emotional wellbeing, relationships, career and bank balance. Through an easy to follow and proven approach, this book will equip you with the best tools to negotiate the moderation process, step-by-step. All aspects of your life will improve with the help of the simple, practical techniques featured, together with relaxing hypnosis recordings that can implant changes at the deepest, healthiest level of your mind.

Alcohol overuse creates multiple health and wellbeing issues for millions of people around the world, but it doesn't have to be that way. By developing self-awareness and using simple behaviour change techniques and specially-designed hypnotherapy recordings, you can feel better about yourself and create a healthier relationship with alcohol.

Having been through the moderation process myself, I understand the road ahead and as such have created this book to empower you to make these changes with confidence and on your own terms, without judgement. This book will show you how you can move forward to the future you really want.

Ten Steps to Drink Less and Live Well is unique because it combines techniques in alcohol moderation, including: tracking monitoring and values recognition. It integrates these methods with the transformative power of hypnotherapy, to produce faster and more long-lasting results.

This book also combines information and hypnosis tracks about how to deal with a lapse, to help if you come across a blip on your journey. This will help you get back on track quickly and to feel optimistic about your broader achievements to date. This book forms part of a wider and much-needed discussion about alcohol issues today. Many people want to cut down on their drinking and are aware of its harmful effects. However, there is still a level of taboo in openly admitting that you have an issue with alcohol and, or want to cut down. I will show you that there is no shame in dealing with your alcohol issues, on the contrary, a great many lives can be improved if not saved, by a shift in societal attitude towards alcohol. Being empowered to change is the greatest gift you can give yourself and this book contributes to that movement.

"When the excessive use of alcohol is removed, you arrive!"

A wonderful life is waiting for you on this journey to moderation mastery. A happy and healthy relationship with yourself and with alcohol is achievable for many people using the simple ten steps featured in this book. Each chapter will guide you through a process of personal discovery, identifying the real reasons why you sometimes drink excessively. You will be amazed and delighted with how much better you feel mentally and physically, as you take control of your habits with permanent lasting change. In addition, towards the end of the book, you can make plans for a healthier and happier future encompassing a holistic approach using my Future Focus Mapping technique.

This book will give you hope, comfort and inspiration on this journey. There is nothing to lose and everything to gain.

Tansy x

Additional support:

You can also access and enjoy your relaxing hypnosis recordings from my website to speed up the positive changes you desire. You will be able to gain additional support and encouragement from myself and others on the same journey via my social media platforms where you can: receive tips; find out about events; and seminars. Also, you can subscribe to my YouTube channel – for free – to access videos about other topics such as deep sleep, to help you relax and unwind further.

CONTENTS LIST

Chapter 3: Step Three: Values; Assess What is Important to You

PART TWO: *Master Your Moderation Skills*

Chapter 4: Step Four: Identify and Deal with Your Overdrinking Triggers

Chapter 5: Step Five: Set Your Limits and Moderation Tools

Chapter 6: Step Six: Take Breaks from Alcohol

PART THREE: Make It Work For The Long Term

Chapter 7: Step Seven: Deal with Any Lapses and Relapses

Chapter 8: Step Eight: Self-Care and Living a Balanced Life

Chapter 9: Step Nine: Need a Helping Hand? Naltrexone and the Sinclair Method

Chapter 10: Step Ten: Create Your Future Focus Map

Case Studies

Chapter 3

Chapter 4

Chapter 5

Chapter 6

PART ONE

Know Your Destination

Chapter 1

STEP ONE:
MODERATION MASTERY;
A JOURNEY OF CHANGE AND GROWTH

"When patterns are broken,
new worlds emerge."

Tuli Kupferberg

Can you imagine how much better your life will be when you regain control of your drinking habits and consume less alcohol? You will wake in the morning feeling fresh and rested after a great night's sleep, ready to enjoy a productive day, feeling positive and energised. Picture yourself making advancements in your career without the after effects of overdrinking hindering your progression. Wouldn't it be great to experience closer relationships with your family, as well as being a great role model to others? Your confidence and self-esteem will improve as you develop a healthier relationship not only with alcohol, but also with yourself too!

When we realise that alcohol is causing us problems, this is a very good time to find strategies to alter our drinking behaviours. This book aims to provide an array of specific and proven practical techniques and ideas to help you cut down and feel much better. It also contains many real-life case studies about alcohol moderation clients who I have worked with in my daily practice. You may find you are able to identify with these experiences. Throughout the book you have access to hypnotherapy recordings to help instil a beneficial outlook relating to moderate drinking and to help you focus on the future that you really want. The recordings work on a subconscious level within your mind, to ensure that drinking becomes less and less important in your life and to increase your ability to think long term about developing a good relationship with alcohol. My approach aims to capitalise on your existing strengths and build your confidence while improving the way you manage your life.

Through time, moderate drinking can become the new normal, and binge drinking part of your past.

My Journey

I was born at 8 o'clock in the morning on Sunday 8 March 1981, in Poole hospital which overlooks the harbour. My mother and father were teachers, originally, from Yorkshire but they moved to the south coast of England after falling in love with Dorset for its dramatic coastline and picturesque rural landscapes. I grew up in a detached 1920s house with a rambling garden in a village six miles west of Poole with my two younger brothers. Our childhood summers were spent sailing in our catamaran around to Old Harry Rocks and Swanage Bay. In the winter we walked in the countryside looking for wild mushrooms and exploring the woods. My early experiences instilled in me a love of nature and I spent a great deal of time picking and arranging flowers to draw and paint. Suffice to say, I had a very happy childhood, and I was both confident and sociable.

However, adolescence brought new challenges and I felt a great deal of pressure to be slim and to conform to ideals of feminine beauty. I was introduced to alcohol during sixth form, when I met up with school friends and went out to the bars of Bournemouth at the weekends. Alcohol made me feel more confident and was a way to let loose and have fun. In 1999, I moved to Bristol to go to university. I loved the city and partying was part of student life, which rolled on into my twenties. I did not have the understanding I have now about the impact of alcohol on my mental health and up to this point alcohol was not causing me problems.

I completed my postgraduate teacher training at Exeter university in 2006 and began my career in an inner-city secondary school in the centre of Bristol. I enjoyed teaching sociology A-level, and I spent the holidays travelling in Europe. It was in 2008, however, that my life took a dramatic shift with the sudden and devastating loss of my younger, middle brother from an accidental drug overdose at the age of 24. Nothing could have prepared me for the catastrophic emotional effect of losing a sibling. It left a gaping hole in my life and affected my childhood memories, since every family photo was a stark reminder of his absence. Perhaps, the fact that I had such an idyllic upbringing made the trauma even more difficult to bear. After his passing, I completed grief therapy, but I found it very difficult to put into words how I was feeling, and I tended to repress my emotions. It was many years later, before I could put the pieces of my life back together.

Anxiety is always something I have been prone to, however after losing my brother I developed more serious issues and also experienced panic attacks. I noticed that my drinking was becoming an unhealthy way to numb my feelings of grief and escape emotional pain. Far from helping, this was complicating the grieving process and creating other problems in my relationships with friends and family. I also realised that the stress of teaching was contributing negatively to my fragile mental health and further compounding the issues. I could no longer try to hide from the negative impact that the overuse of alcohol was having on my life, and I was ready for a change.

I started looking into options for the treatment of 'alcohol use disorder' apart from the traditionally prescribed routes such as Alcoholics Anonymous. I looked at hypnotherapy as a tool for behaviour change, which I found to be totally transformative.

Hypnotherapy raised my self-esteem and allowed me to think more clearly and calmly. During this time, I successfully cut down my alcohol intake. My mental health improved immeasurably along with my personal and professional life. I also had the mental clarity and emotional equilibrium required to work through my grief, build my confidence and find happiness once again. It was this experience that inspired me to train as a hypnotherapist and help others on their path to wellness.

I realised that If I was having these issues there must be many other people who want to make a change but feel stuck in a cycle of overdrinking. The more I researched the treatment of alcohol issues, the more I appreciated why so many people were reluctant to pursue the current routes. *Ten Steps to Drink Less and Live Well* was born out of my frustration with the existing support available for those people who have alcohol issues. It is now my pleasure and privilege to help others move on from their past, find freedom from overdrinking and enhance their whole lives.

My Approach

The key premise of my approach is that moderate drinking is a practical and reasonable goal for those people who face less severe drinking issues. I recognise that there are a great many differences in peoples' overdrinking behaviours and the suggestions in this book allow for your own interpretation of what you find most helpful. You can apply them at your own discretion. The aim is for you to create a toolkit of strategies that work for you. The main aspects of the change process, as featured in this book, include the following:

- Assess whether moderation is right for you.
- Tune in with your personal values.
- Master your moderation skill set.
- Deal with any lapses.
- Make plans for your future.

By following the same ten step path, exactly the same as I and countless numbers of my clients have taken, you will: sleep better; save money; feel calmer and happier; and enjoy being more connected to the people around you. By using the tried and tested methods featured in this book, as well as harnessing the transformative power of hypnotherapy, you can create a better future and really enjoy the journey along the way.

Chapter 2

STEP TWO:
IS MODERATION SUITABLE FOR YOU?

*"It is not as much about who you used to be,
as it is about who you choose to be."*

Sanhita Baruah

The purpose of this chapter is to give you an understanding of the range of alcohol issues that exist in our society. When we locate ourselves on this spectrum, we can assess the likelihood of success in moderating our drinking, in other words, drinking safely. This chapter will open your eyes to evidence-based research, which demonstrates how there is a much greater proportion of the population for whom moderation is suitable, in contrast to what the mass media and popular wisdom would have you believe.

Many people find it highly motivating to know about other people who have effectively moderated their drinking habits and who have been in similar situations. You will have a chance to identify where you fit on the continuum of alcohol use disorder. By doing so, you can be fully informed of your current situation and the likely outcome of your efforts to decrease your alcohol intake on a permanent basis. The wonderful and empowering news is that you will learn about the spectrum of decreasing alcohol use and how you can transition to a much safer usage. The research and statistics come from both the United Kingdom and international sources to give you the broadest perspective on these worldwide topics.

Are You Ready for a Surprise?

People who have had mild to moderate alcohol use disorder but have not been severely physically addicted, can bring their alcohol use to healthy levels through moderation techniques. It is also unlikely that you will be reading this book if you fall into the most severe bracket. Current statistics indicate that

approximately 20 percent of the UK population are drinking at harmful levels

approximately 20 percent of the UK population are drinking at harmful levels and only one percent of that group is physically addicted. According to research that we will explore in this chapter, moderation is a viable option for the great majority of problem drinkers. This is fantastic news for many people who would like to transition from heavier usage.

If you choose to embark on the moderation path it is a transformational journey, which will not always be easy, but it will be the best gift you have ever given yourself and your loved ones. You will gain more self-confidence; have a greater sense of achievement in overcoming this obstacle; be more productive and successful; have closer relationships; and have increased health and wellbeing now and in the future.

Our society, historically, has had a strange relationship with alcohol; moving between puritanism and hedonism. One hand often berating and judging people harshly for drunkenness, yet also glamorising alcohol at every turn. Television, films and the mass media often feature characters who are either doing really well in life and drinking alcohol or people who are at rock bottom and drinking alcohol, with very little in between. In fact, there is a much broader range of ways in which people use and abuse alcohol. This waxes and wanes according to what is going on in people's lives at the time. This has led to a disconnect between conventional wisdom and what research data demonstrates. There is a great deal of evidence showing that large numbers of people with alcohol issues learn to moderate their intake successfully without treatment. The reason we don't know about this comes down to history and politics. This chapter gives a very brief history of how alcohol use has been viewed and how this affects public perception and the treatments available.

The Prohibition Era and the Twelve Step Movement

Alcoholics Anonymous continues to be the dominant avenue for people with alcohol issues in the UK today, and indeed across the globe. It was founded in 1935, by Bill Wilson and Dr Bob Smith, during the post prohibition era in America. At the time, there were very few options for people in need of assistance in relation to alcohol misuse and it is commendable that they came up with a list of actions that helped people to become abstinent. Prohibition was a movement in the USA that created a ban on the production, importation and sale of alcohol from 1920 to 1933. It was driven by religious groups who considered alcohol a threat to the nation, both socially and economically. At this time, heavy drinking was perceived as a moral failure and the medical profession treated it as incurable and lethal. The Twelve Steps were first used as the roadmap to alcohol abstinence, to promote a mainly moral cure, which centres on confession, repentance, atonement and turning one's will over to a higher power.

Read through the following Twelve Steps and see what you think.

The Twelve Steps to Alcohol Abstinence

The following are the original twelve steps published by Alcoholics Anonymous (AA) in 1935.

1. We admit we were powerless over alcohol; that our lives had become unmanageable.

2. We believe that a power greater than ourselves could restore us to sanity.

3. We made a decision to turn our will, and our lives, over to the care of God as we understand Him.

4. We made a searching and moral inventory of ourselves.

5. We admitted to God, to ourselves, and to another human being the exact nature of our wrongs.

6. We were entirely ready to have God remove all these defects of character.

7. We humbly ask Him to remove our shortcomings.

8. We made a list of all persons we had harmed and became willing to make amends to them all.

9. We made direct amends to such people wherever possible, except when to do so would injure them or other people.

10. We continued to take a personal inventory, and when we were wrong, promptly admitted it.

11. We sought through prayer and meditation, to improve our conscious contact with God as we understood him, praying for knowledge of His will for us, and the power to carry that out.

12. Having a spiritual awakening as a result of these steps, we tried to carry this message to other alcoholics and to practice these principles in all our affairs.

It is interesting to note that AA was originally intended for the most severe alcohol abuser, yet the Twelve Step philosophy has filtered into a majority of treatment programmes around the world and remains as the 'go to' recommendation for all people with alcohol issues. According to the latest statistics, there are about five thousand AA meetings running in the UK today. It is also the basis of approximately 90 percent of the rehab treatment programmes currently operating in the USA. For people who have been severely physically addicted to alcohol, AA can provide a free source of support. However, it is clear that there is currently a lack of other treatment options for people who fall into the much larger bracket of mild to moderate alcohol issues, and therefore, for whom moderation is a viable alternative.

The Disease Theory of Addiction

The founders of AA did not say that alcoholism was a disease but rather that these people were drinking to fill a void in their lives. The disease model that is put forward by AA nowadays was adopted by the administration at a later stage. Positioning alcohol issues as a disease has its problems, yet it is also helpful because alcohol use disorder came some way towards being viewed as a medical rather than a moral or social failing.

In 2018, The American National Institute of Drug Abuse defined addiction as; *"A chronic, relapsing disorder characterised by compulsive drug seeking, continued use despite harmful consequences, and long-lasting changes in the brain. It is considered both a complex brain disorder and a mental illness. Addiction is the most severe form of substance use disorders, and is a mental illness caused by a repeated misuse of a substance or substances."*

Problematic alcohol use could now be handled within the healthcare field and the government provided funding for prevention and assistance. Society began to take on board the fact that undesirable behaviours from severe alcohol use were not about a simple bad habit, but that there were many more complex elements of a psychological disorder. The most recent United States Surgeon General's Report in 2016, put forward the idea that addiction to alcohol is a chronic brain disease that has the potential for recurrence and recovery. Cyndi Turner, author of *The Clinician's Guide to Alcohol Moderation* states that only very severe alcohol use disorders should carry the label of addiction because it is very different from problematic alcohol use.

A Lucrative Industry

It is also relevant to understand that addiction treatment is a more than US$35 billion dollar industry in America, in which venture capitalists and private equity firms, together with all manner of investors place their financial interests. It is a great deal more lucrative for individuals to be placed in inpatient facilities. In this way, there is a vested interest in this often-relapsing condition because the consumer is contending with a condition that may require several bouts of expensive treatment. Current estimates place rehabilitation treatment anywhere up to £10,000 a week in the UK. It may be argued that it pays for investors to label a person as an alcoholic because the greater the level and length of care, the more expensive it is, and the greater profit can be made. After inpatient facilities have been attended, there will potentially be aftercare and outpatient interventions. If you would like to learn more about this topic, *The Business of Recovery* is an informative online documentary that you can watch.

Alcohol Use Disorder

The term 'alcoholic' is not a clinical term. In fact, it is a word used since the mid-1800s to denote a person who is experiencing alcohol issues. The way in which professionals such as psychiatrists and doctors currently make a diagnosis is by using the Diagnostic and Statistical Manual of Mental Disorders (DSM 5) which now classifies alcohol use disorder as mild, moderate or severe.

People on the continuum without a physical dependence, such as mild to moderate use disorder can, with the right tools, skills, and support, learn to drink alcohol at safer levels. A large number of people experience alcohol use disorder at the mild to moderate end of the spectrum. This group has the potential to reduce their drinking to much safer levels on a permanent basis and live much happier and more fulfilling lives.

You now have a chance to assess where you think you currently are on this spectrum.

Alcohol use disorder can be classified as a problem in relation to alcohol consumption, which leads to significant impairment or distress, as indicated by a minimum of at least two of the following points during a twelve-month time frame. The information below is taken directly from the DSM 5.

1. Alcohol is often taken in larger amounts or over a longer period than was intended.

2. There is a persistent desire or unsuccessful efforts to cut down or control alcohol use.

3. A great deal of time is spent on activities necessary to obtain alcohol, use alcohol, or recover from its effects.

4. Craving, strong desire or urge to use alcohol.

5. Recurrent alcohol use resulting in a failure to fulfil major role obligations at work school or home.

6. Continued alcohol use despite having persistent or recurrent social or interpersonal problems caused or exacerbated by the effect of alcohol.

7. Important social, occupational, or recreational activities are given up or reduced because of alcohol use.

8. Recurrent alcohol use in situations that are physically hazardous.

9. Alcohol use is continued despite a knowledge of having a persistent or recurrent physical problem that is likely to be exacerbated by alcohol.

10. Tolerance, that is defined by either of the following: a) a need for markedly increased amounts of alcohol to achieve intoxication or desired effect; or b) a markedly diminished effect with the continued use of the same amount of alcohol.

II. Withdrawal as shown by either of the following: a) the characteristic withdrawal syndrome for alcohol (see next section below, about withdrawal symptoms); or b) alcohol (or a closely-related substance, such as benzodiazepine) is taken to relieve or avoid withdrawal symptoms.

Disorder Definitions

- Mild alcohol use disorder: two or three symptoms present.
- Moderate alcohol use disorder: four to five symptoms present.
- Severe alcohol use disorder: six or more symptoms present.

If you fall into the mild to moderate bracket, moderation may be suitable for you.

Withdrawal from Alcohol

Many people face confusion with the difference between a hangover, which potentially includes: grogginess; nausea; being sick; gastric distress; and tiredness; with *bone fide* alcohol withdrawal. It is vital to understand that true alcohol withdrawal can be fatal. True withdrawal symptoms are a clear indication of a physical dependence on alcohol and it is unlikely for these people to be able to drink safely again. A person suffering from any of the symptoms below, not attributable to another medical condition, will have to go to the accident and emergency department to have a medically supervised detox.

A. Cessation of, or reduction in alcohol use, that has been heavy or prolonged.

B. Two or more of the following, developing within several hours to a few days after the cessation or reduction in alcohol use as described in criterion A.

1. Autonomic hyperactivity (for example, sweating or pulse rate greater than 100bpm)
2. Increased hand tremor
3. Insomnia
4. Nausea or vomiting
5. Transient visual, auditory hallucinations or illusions
6. Psychomotor agitation
7. Anxiety
8. Generalised tonic-chronic seizures; formerly known as grand mal seizures.

C. The signs and symptoms in criterion B cause clinically-significant distress or impairment in social, occupational or other areas of functioning.

D. The signs and symptoms are not attributable to another medical condition and are not better explained by another mental disorder, including intoxication or withdrawal from another substance.

Types of Drinkers in the UK

The latest figures from the Office of National Statistics indicate that there are 67 million people residing in the UK. The diagram below paints a picture of the types of drinkers who make up the population. Consider this image and decide, which drinker are you?

TYPES OF DRINKERS IN THE UK

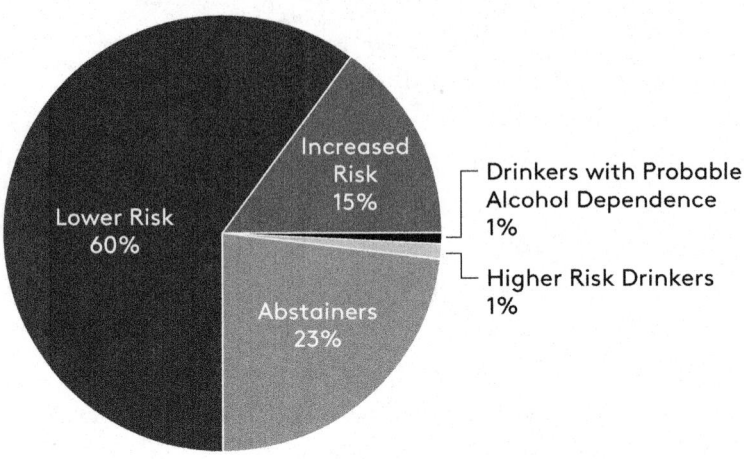

Based on data from the Alcohol Toolkit Study for December 2020–November 2021 for England

Categories Defined

Abstainers 23%

Lower Risk 60% (14 units per week)

Increased Risk 15% (35 units per week for women and 50 for men)

Higher Risk Drinkers 1% (more than 50 units per week)

Drinkers with Probable Alcohol Dependence 1%

What Does Moderation Mean?

Moderation has been defined as low-risk drinking. According to the UK Department of Health, their current recommendation is 14 units for both men and women spread across three or more days. This is approximately a bottle and a half of wine or 14 single measures of a spirit.

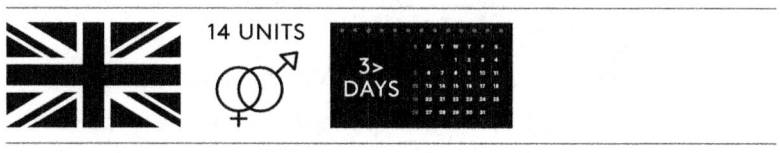

According to the Dietary Guidelines for Americans, drinking moderately is defined as two standard drinks or less per day for men or one standard drink or less in a day for women. A standard drink is defined as 12oz of beer at 5% abv, 8oz of malt liquor at 7% abv, 5oz of wine at 12% abv or 1.5 oz of distilled spirits at 40% (80 proof) abv.

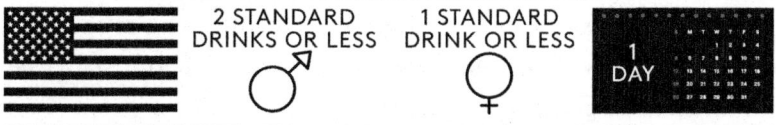

Moderation Management is a well-known behavioural change programme in the harm reduction field. It defines a moderate drinker as a person with the following characteristics.

• Considers an occasional drink to be a small though enjoyable part of life.

- Has hobbies, interests and other ways to enjoy life that do not involve alcohol.
- Usually has friends who are moderate drinkers or non-drinkers.
- Usually does not drink longer than an hour or two on any particular occasion.
- Usually does not exceed the 0.55 percent blood alcohol concentration drinking limit.
- Usually does not drink faster than one drink per half hour.
- Feels comfortable with his or her use of alcohol, never drinking in secret or spending much time thinking about drinking or planning to drink.

These guidelines are helpful in allowing us to think about where we want to aim for, in terms of moderation, and we will look at the refining of your goals in subsequent chapters. We will also be exploring many strategies that have worked for other people, and you can enjoy planning what is healthy and sustainable for you.

A moderate drinker is generally someone who enjoys the relaxing and social benefits of an occasional drink or two, while minimising negative consequences. Drinking is in proportion with the rest of their life in that it does not dominate and there are other sources of interest, joy and stimulation. Many people report becoming so much happier and content in other areas of their life and have the time and inclination to develop new interests and passions.

EXERCISE

Assess Where You are Currently at on the Alcohol Use Disorder Spectrum

Q	SYMPTOMS	YES	NO
1	Alcohol is often taken in larger amounts or over a longer period than was intended.		
2	There is a persistent desire or unsuccessful efforts to cut down or control alcohol use.		
3	A great deal of time is spent on activities necessary to obtain alcohol, use alcohol, or recover from its effects.		
4	Craving, strong desire or urge to use alcohol.		
5	Recurrent alcohol use resulting in a failure to fulfil major role obligations at work.		
6	Continued alcohol use despite having persistent or recurrent social or interpersonal problems caused or exacerbated by the effect of alcohol.		
7	Important social, occupational, or recreational activities are given up or reduced because of alcohol use.		
8	Recurrent alcohol use in situations that are physically hazardous.		

9   Alcohol use is continued despite a
    knowledge of having a persistent or
    recurrent physical problem that is likely
    to be exacerbated by alcohol.

10 Tolerance, that is defined by either of the
    following:

a. a need for markedly increased amounts of
    alcohol to achieve intoxication or desired
    effect; or

b. a markedly diminished effect with the
    continued use of the same amount of
    alcohol.

11 Withdrawal as shown by either of the
    following:

a. the characteristic withdrawal syndrome for
    alcohol (see page 16, 17 about withdrawal
    symptoms); or

b. alcohol (or a closely-related substance, such
    as benzodiazepine) is taken to relieve or
    avoid withdrawal symptoms.

CURRENT RESULT	MILD	MOD	SEVERE
Mild alcohol use disorder: two or three symptoms present.	☐	☐	☐
Moderate alcohol use disorder: four to five symptoms present.	☐	☐	☐
Severe alcohol use disorder: six or more symptoms present.	☐	☐	☐

Well done! Come back and see how things change in six months or so. So many of my clients show significant changes for the better – You can do it!

LATER RESULT	MILD	MOD	SEVERE
Mild alcohol use disorder: two or three symptoms present.	☐	☐	☐
Moderate alcohol use disorder: four to five symptoms present.	☐	☐	☐
Severe alcohol use disorder: six or more symptoms present.	☐	☐	☐

The Evidence for Moderation

Conventional wisdom may have you believe that if you suffer with alcohol issues on any level then abstinence-based recovery is the only option since it is an incurable disease that will get worse over time. However, as you will discover, the evidence reveals a different picture. The eminent researchers, Linda and Mark Sobell of the Addiction Research Foundation of Toronto, Canada in 1995, after nearly three decades of study into alcohol use, concluded that if you are someone who does not have a serious physical dependence you can implement moderation techniques and be successful in the long term.

A national five-year study in the US of 43,000 people sponsored by the Institute of Alcohol Abuse and Alcoholism, concluding in 2005, highlighted evidence that the majority of people can change their drinking habits through education in a non-confrontational manner relating to impact and risks of overdrinking. Interestingly, they also found that over a lifetime 30 percent of adults will experience an alcohol use disorder, yet 70 per cent of those people will transition to safe drinking patterns over time.

The World Health Organisation (WHO) undertook research in 1996 with 1,490 heavy but non-dependent drinkers at ten differing locations across the world who had each received a short intervention relating to alcohol. The group was monitored nine months after receiving the support and information and it was discovered that the group had managed to curtail their consumption by about one third.

Another revealing study was the *The Birmingham Untreated Heavy Drinkers Project,* conducted by The Department of Health UK and published in 2009. The 259 participants recruited referred to themselves as 'drinking like fish'. At intervals during a ten-year period, they were interviewed periodically but not given any form of treatment. Interestingly, at the end of this time 28 of the people who previously were very heavy drinkers were not drinking at all and 53 were drinking within the government's recommended levels for safer usage. Those who moderated outnumbered those who were abstinent by nearly two to one.

It is also important to consider, as we often see with family and friends, that people can move up and down the alcohol use disorder spectrum. We have all heard about someone we know who may have suffered a breakup or traumatic experience and for a while they turn to alcohol to drown their sorrows. They may do this for a period of time and when they recover, they resume more moderate drinking patterns. Furthermore, we see that in many cases young people at university may drink heavily in their late teens to early twenties. At that time, they may have fallen into the classification for alcohol use disorder. Yet, they become more moderate as they move through the later life stages. Did they attend an alcohol rehabilitation and declare themselves an addict? Highly unlikely.

Research conducted in a *Drinking Patterns and Drinking Problems* survey by Cahalan and Room discovered that even in the case of a great majority of people with drinking issues who are untreated, such problems decrease precipitously by the age of 30 years old. In this case, many individuals cut back or eradicate the problem drinking with age. Further to this, Stanton Peele Phd, author of the book *Truth About Addiction and Recovery*, points out that it is not only college students or those with mild drinking problems who cut back over time. "Maturing out occurs at all stages of the life cycle up to, and including, old age." Milton and Gross, the medical researchers who coined the term Alcohol Dependence Syndrome (ADS), were enlightened by the fact that most people with alcohol issues, "Free themselves from alcohol dependence and the withdrawal process when the associated desire and drive to drink collide with the totality of the individual and the whole of life." Put another way, sooner or later a person sees more reasons to cease such problematic drinking than to continue it. Overall, it is encouraging to see from the research that moderation is a reasonable and attainable goal for many people with mild or moderate alcohol problems.

The Continuum of Decreasing Alcohol Use

There is a continuum of alcohol use which many people transition down on a regular basis to safer alcohol use. A generally accepted belief is that if we run into any issue with alcohol then it is a one-way ticket to disaster. However, it is often the exact opposite and many more people need to know about this to be inspired and empowered to take positive action.

READER REFLECTION EXERCISE

Transition to Safer Drinking;
An Overview of the Moderation Journey

- Where will your drinking habits be in six months' to a year's time?

_____

_____

- In what ways will your life improve as you cut down on alcohol?

_____

_____

THE CONTINUUM OF DECREASING ALCOHOL USE

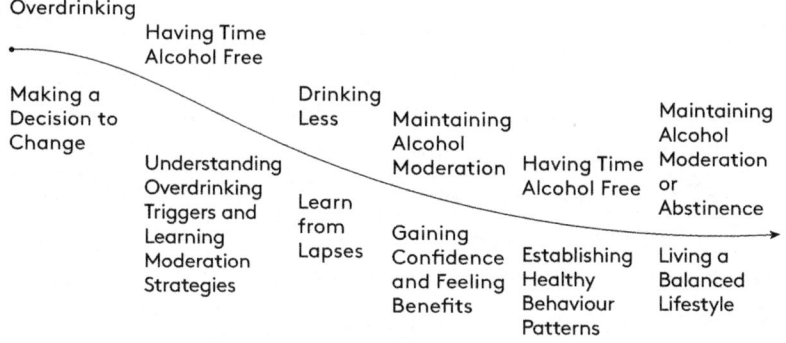

With kind permission of Cyndi Turner, LGSW, LSATP, MAC, adapted from *The Clinician's Guide to Alcohol Moderation*

The spectrum above gives an overview of the moderation journey as detailed in the rest of this book. The stages may not all happen in this sequential order, but it demonstrates the general trajectory of behaviour modification. At the start is your recognition of the overdrinking and your decision to change. Alcohol-free time is recommended at this point to reset your tolerance and to have time unclouded in which to strengthen your resolve for change and develop sober coping strategies. Next comes self-knowledge of overdrinking triggers and the acquisition of your alcohol moderation skill set. Learning from lapses is also important to refine an understanding of triggers as your journey progresses. In time, instances of overdrinking will decrease and your confidence will be on the rise as positive behaviour patterns are established and maintained.

Alcohol is a good servant but a terrible master.

Living a balanced lifestyle is an integral part of sustaining a moderate existence. Time alcohol free where appropriate, can be used at your discretion throughout your journey during times of stress, or after a lapse to restore emotional equilibrium. The other end of the continuum is abstinence and Cyndi Turner, author of *The Clinician's Guide to Alcohol Moderation,* indicates that about one third of those people who embark on a moderation journey eventually choose abstinence. Some people report that they feel that their lives are better without alcohol and ultimately, decide to go alcohol free. Once you have cut down you will be able to decide the part, if any, that alcohol plays in your life. You may be content moderating, or you may decide to abstain. Either way you will be happier and healthier.

Your Way Forward

Now you have a good grasp of where you are on the alcohol use disorder spectrum. Isn't it wonderful to know that you have options and choices about where you can take your life next? It can be daunting to embark on a process of change, but fear not, you have everything to gain and nothing to lose. This is the start of a wonderful journey to freedom!

It was said by the late journalist and author Christopher Hitchens, that "Alcohol is a good servant but a terrible master." This is a poignant quote because we can, at certain points in life, and often unknowingly, let alcohol take the driving seat. But you are not powerless to change. The more you develop your self-awareness, the more you will understand your personal triggers for overdrinking and come to deal with life more effectively through healthier coping strategies.

Trust the process and yourself. Make a commitment to yourself right now to begin the journey of change. Stick with it – through thick and thin – to reach a point where you feel happy with yourself and your use of alcohol.

Please go to the webpage www.drinklesslivewell.com to access the hypnosis recording that compliments this chapter entitled; **Draw Strength and Step into Your Power.**

Chapter 3

STEP THREE:
VALUES; ASSESS WHAT IS
IMPORTANT TO YOU

*"No one can persuade another to change.
Each of us guards a gate of change that can
only be opened from the inside."*

Marilyn Ferguson

A core principle of mastering moderation is tuning in to your deepest held values, those which are in opposition to overdrinking because this creates the pressure to change. A value, simply put, is something important that you believe is worth striving for in your life. As a human being, we make hundreds of decisions every day about every aspect of our life. The lived experience is complicated and multifaceted and we can be pulled in many directions, some of them not always positive. When we use our values to make decisions, we make a deliberate choice to focus on what is important to us. As you will no doubt discover along the way, a moderation journey isn't simply about cutting down on alcohol, it is about creating your best and happiest, healthiest and most fulfilling life. Living in alignment with your core values is a dependable way to move in this direction and I will show you how.

Very often our values may lie dormant as Stanton Peele, a senior psychologist in the field of harm reduction and author of *The Truth About Addiction,* pointed out. He said that if the behaviour we are trying to move away from were so contradictory to our value system, then perhaps we may not have got entangled in it in the first place. However, Peele highlights that, "In the fever pitch of addiction, as when embarking on a love affair, people forget what is important to them." An example might be the mother who dearly loves her children but is overdrinking to cope with the stress of parenthood. In the moment, the alcohol acts as a temporary remedy for the emotional discomfort she is experiencing. However, it is hurting what is most important to her by negatively affecting her judgement when it comes to her parenting practices. She is acting in accordance with her emotional response to alleviate the stress and not according to her values.

In this chapter you have the chance to reevaluate and tune in with your core values, those that are most connected with your sense of self. This process not only helps illuminate and strengthen your connection to the elements of your life that are most important, it also helps build your personal agency in relation to that which you will not sacrifice to the detrimental effects of alcohol. When we make these judgements with more clarity, the other parts of the journey fall into place a great deal more easily.

Reactivity Versus Proactivity

Pause for a moment here and ask yourself the following question.

- How are you feeling right now?
- Think about your mood, are you happy, sad, irritated?
- How is your mind working?
- Is it quick and responsive or are you feeling sleepy?

This ability to know how we feel is unique to human beings and is called self-awareness. We are separated from animals by the fact that we have self-awareness; the ability to think about our own thought processes. This permits us to evaluate and learn from the experiences of others as well as our own, and this can aid us in breaking destructive behaviour cycles relating to overdrinking. With this unique capacity we can consider our patterns of behaviour to understand if they are reality-based (what we are facing in the moment) or value-based reactions to a stimulus. It is important to remember that you are not your habits, and you can replace old patterns of self-defeating behaviour. I witness this all the time in my practice as clients develop their self-awareness and self-knowledge by reflecting on behaviours that are not benefiting them and choose a new healthier and happier path. And you can too!

TAMARA, 36, USED HER VALUES AS A COMPASS TO MASTER MODERATION

Tamara was a classic binge drinker in her teens and twenties, which rolled into her thirties and started to affect her personal relationships and professional life. She was unhappy in her job as a nurse, anxious and drinking to cope with stress and negative emotions. At university, she had a good social life and her focus had been on friendships and living life in the moment. In her early thirties, she met her now husband and moved to a new, livelier, bigger city to be with him. At first, it was exciting to live somewhere new and go out and drink and socialise. Many of her university friends were there too, but her wellbeing was suffering, and the fast-paced lifestyle compounded her drinking and mental health issues.

When she went out with friends, she ended up drinking far too much and not eating, which meant it took her days to recover and she was blighted by high anxiety. She often resorted to 'the hair of the dog' the following lunchtime or evening to feel better. She had a pre-existing anxiety disorder and at that time also suffered panic attacks. On the surface her life looked good, she was intelligent, caring and very sociable, but delving a bit deeper, it was clear that life was spiralling quickly into worse and worse drinking related problems. She could no longer ignore the signs and really valued her relationship with her partner who wasn't happy about it all. She wanted to progress in her relationship, but she was stuck in a cycle of overdrinking followed by shame, anxiety and regret.

When Tamara tried to cut down on her own, at first, she had no success. Anxiety was a barrier to making long-lasting changes to her lifestyle and curbing the overdrinking because she was stuck in a negative spiral of self-medication. Her journey back to health involved Cognitive Behavioural Therapy (often known as CBT) for anxiety and using a structured approach to cutting down through moderation techniques and hypnotherapy to boost her self-esteem because she was at a pretty low ebb. Tamara found that determining her values was central to the change in her relationship with alcohol. After working on her values, she developed a clearer understanding of the aspects of her life that were most important to her. These elements centred on: health; love; family; and education. Tuning in with the value of love she realised that her relationship with her partner was central to her happiness, and she did not want to endanger this with destructive overdrinking. The negative impact of alcohol on her mental health was an inescapable fact and she could not stand the anxiety and negative emotions that were exacerbated by heavy drinking. Tamara made excellent progress and in time cut down on the instances of overdrinking and rebuilt her life. Tamara changed careers and the amazing thing was that she was able to move on positively and strengthen her relationships. The heavy drinking problem was a passing phase and although she had to be aware of it in the future as she knew that she could be vulnerable in triggering situations, she now has the skills to manage such occurrences. Tamara is now a stable moderate drinker.

By studying and considering your values you will be encouraged to open the gate of change and growth. As Stephen Covey, author of *The Seven Habits of Highly Effective People,* helpfully reminds us, "Have patience with yourself, self-growth is tender; it is holy ground. There is no greater investment." When it comes to alcohol moderation there is rarely a quick fix, but I promise you that you will feel the benefits and see immediate payoffs that will inspire you to progress. Celebrate all positive changes, however small, over time these will accumulate and lead to huge advancements in your personal growth.

Stimulus-Response Theory

It may be accurate to say that our behaviour is to some extent influenced by conditioning and conditions. However, to conclude that we are determined by it, that we have no control, creates a quite different conception of our potential life journey. There are three dominant theories of behaviour.

Genetic Determinism

The theory that behaviour comes from genetic makeup that is passed down through the family and accounts for the behavioural traits and outcomes of an individual.

Psychic Determinism

The idea that cognition, behaviour and decision-making are a result of childhood experiences that influence the structure of one's character.

Environmental Determinism

A theory which suggests that social forces within the environment a person is exposed to controls their thinking, feeling, striving and behaviour.

Each of these behaviour maps is based on the stimulus response theory that we may associate with the theory of Pavlov's dogs. This theory on classical conditioning denotes that we are conditioned to respond in a certain way to a particular stimulus as shown in the diagram below.

REACTIVE RESPONSE DIAGRAM

Stimulus   •⎯⎯⎯⎯⎯⎯⎯⎯⟶ Response

With kind permission of Franklin Covey, adapted from *The Seven Habits of Highly Effective People* by Steven Covey

---

However, we have to ask ourselves; how accurate and functional are such theories that try to determine our behavior? Many people argue that they are disempowering and create self-fulfilling prophecies.

In exploring such questions, it is helpful to look at the case of the Jewish psychiatrist Victor Frankl in his autobiography *Man's Search for Meaning,* detailing his harrowing experiences when he was imprisoned in the death camps of Nazi Germany for three years. Many of his close family members were killed and he suffered experiences that were so abhorrent to one's sense of decency that we would shudder to repeat them. His parents, his brother and his wife, who was a nurse, died in the concentration camps or were sent to the gas chambers. His daily life was perpetually in a state of not knowing if he would live, die, or be shovelling the ashes of those who were fated.

Alone and naked in a tiny cell, he began to further develop his awareness of what he described as one of the "last of the human freedoms," the only aspect of himself that his Nazi captors could not remove from him. He had written about these concepts before he arrived at the camp and was now applying them to his experiences. The guards had the ability to control his whole environment and they could do what they wanted to his physical body. However, Frankl was himself a human being who had the capacity to view as an observer, his particular involvement in the concentration camp. He understood that at a basic level his identity was intact. He could make a decision about how his experiences were going to affect him. In the space in between what happened to him and his response to it, was the freedom and power to choose a proactive course of action.

When he was in the camp, Frankl visualised himself in different experiences, such as lecturing to his students after his release from the camp. In his mind, he described himself in the classroom, teaching his students on the very experiences he was having in the death camps of his torture. Through a series of disciplines, including: mental; moral; and emotional, primarily using his memory and imagination, he exercised this tiny amount of freedom until it became bigger and bigger, until he had greater levels of freedom than his German captors. They had the liberty of their environment, but he ultimately had the greatest freedom of his internal power to exercise his options. Frankl became an inspiration to other people around him and to several of the German guards. One particular guard depended on Frankl for advice about his marriage. During these experiences Frankl employed the unique human capability of self-awareness to call to action a key principle concerning the nature of man. He helped people to find meaning in their existence even when they were suffering the horrendous indignities of the prison camps.

"Between stimulus and response there is a space. In that space is our power to choose our response."

Victor Frankl

Through pausing and observing what happens in the space between stimulus and response, it is possible to cope more effectively with everything that is going on around you. You can remain calm and choose a better response that is more productive for the situation at hand. By taking time to recognise and take control of that space between stimulus and response, we can live in alignment with a deeper value-driven purpose, as detailed in the diagram below.

PROACTIVE CHOICES DIAGRAM

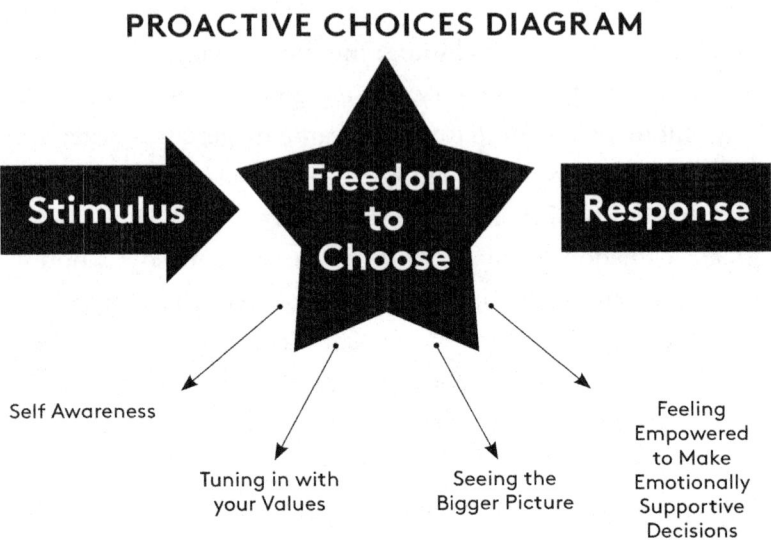

Stimulus → Freedom to Choose → Response

Self Awareness

Tuning in with your Values

Seeing the Bigger Picture

Feeling Empowered to Make Emotionally Supportive Decisions

With kind permission of Franklin Covey, adapted from *The Seven Habits of Highly Effective People* by Steven Covey

JANE, 45, REAPED THE BENEFITS OF DEVELOPING HER SELF-AWARENESS

Along with tuning in with her underpinning value system, applying the space between stimulus and response philosophy was advantageous for one of my clients in the early stages of her moderation journey. Jane was a high-achieving businesswoman who was recently divorced and lived with her two children. She had enjoyed socialising during university and had a successful career. After a busy day at work, Jane drank wine at home and had seen her intake rise substantially over the last few years. Feeling tired, anxious and overwhelmed by the situation, Jane decided she wanted to change this pattern and regain control of her alcohol consumption and her life. She worked diligently to tune in with her value system, which revealed one of her core values as family or in her words 'being the best mum she could be'. Jane felt that her drinking was interfering with her ability to manage her son's behaviour, which could be challenging. Crystalising her focus on the value of family and its incompatibility with overdrinking helped her moderation plans fall into place. One of the first simple actions Jane implemented was to introduce alcohol-free days, which lowered her monthly intake by forty units early on – the equivalent of four bottles of wine. This was an enormous step forward from her previous daily drinking. Stress at work in her high-pressure and responsible position was a trigger for opening a bottle of wine at the end of the day. Hypnotherapy helped Jane to relax and reduce stress and she reported that it allowed her to create mental space between a stressful situation and her response. Prior to this, the stimulus was stress at work or a parenting issue and her response was to drink, believing it would help her relax.

In fact, she found it didn't actually make her feel better when she drank on a stress trigger, she felt more keyed up and less able to deal with the situation at hand. She learned that if she were to pause and observe herself in the moment, this self-awareness allowed her to step outside of herself, as a witness or observer to the situation. In this moment, she had the freedom to choose, and this realisation provided her with the opportunity for personal growth and development. Jane was in the early stages of the moderation journey, yet with these insights she experienced significant improvements that were motivating and inspiring. As a result, she developed increased control and empowerment in her relationship with herself and with alcohol.

Find Meaning and Direction in Your Life

Frankl believed that human beings are motivated by something called a; 'Will to Meaning,' which is the desire to find purpose in life. He argued that life can have meaning even in the most miserable of circumstances and that the motivation for living comes from finding that meaning.

MIKE, 38, PROGRESSED RAPIDLY ONCE HE HAD DISCOVERED DIRECTION IN HIS LIFE

Mike worked in the alcohol-saturated media industry and since university had been prone to bouts of binge drinking that he found affected his energy levels as well as his self-esteem. As a highly motivated and determined young man he had made marked progress in his moderation journey and had significantly cut down on the instances of overdrinking. He undertook substantial work in tackling the issue by identifying his overdrinking triggers, as well as planning ahead and risk assessing social engagements. He also tested out moderation techniques, such as: delaying drinking; gaining support from friends; drinking lower alcohol options; and charting his progress on a wall planner. He also took one or two months off alcohol, which helped him realise how much more energy he had when he wasn't recovering from a heavy session of drinking each week. Mike identified times when he could moderate safely and times when it was best to avoid alcohol. He enjoyed the moderate drinking experiences more and more. It was amazing to see his confidence grow as he transitioned into much greater levels of health and wellbeing.

A key part of Mike's positive evolution was brought about by assessing and tuning in with his core values, which helped guide him in his day-to-day decision-making processes. After completing the values activity Mike discovered one of the core principles that resonated with him was that of personal growth and development, and engaging with this value helped further his positive trajectory. He had always been truly enthusiastic about all aspects of Italian culture. He loved the weather, the food, the architecture, the relaxed way of life and was saving up to buy a property in the southern region. He spent his spare time learning the language and researching the new life that he was planning for the future. He found as he cut down on alcohol, he had more energy to devote to these projects that were a source of joy and central to his identity. Having this stronger connection to a meaningful purpose allowed Mike to increase his motivation in relation to his moderation journey. The more time he spent on it, the more he enjoyed the project and engaged with his aspiration. In this way, he was much less likely to be swayed by a short-term impulse to binge drink because he had plans for himself that overdrinking would interfere with. Mike was looking forward to greater accomplishments. He realised through this process that establishing the desire and the hope of achieving substantial goals is pre-eminent in eliminating overdrinking.

YOUR VALUES REFLECTION EXERCISE

Our values reflect what we find meaningful within our lives. They are the aspects that you care for deep down and that you believe to be important. Values can sometimes lie dormant and it can be helpful to get back in touch with them through exercises such as the one in this chapter. This can allow us to lead a more fulfilling and happy life.

Everyone's values are unique and they can alter during our lifetime. An example might be health, which requires a lifetime's effort, with a specific related goal of taking exercise classes each week. Have a look at the list on the next page and think about what makes a meaningful life for you. By the end of the exercise you will have narrowed down five values that feel most essential to the life you want to live.

YOUR VALUES REFLECTIONS EXERCISE

1. Get in touch with your core values. From the selection below note down or underline the words that most resonate with you personally.

Acceptance	Contentment	Gratitude	Originality
Accountability	Courage	Happiness	Passion
Achievement	Curiosity	Health	Performance
Active	Daring	Honesty	Personal
Adventure	Decisiveness	Humour	Development
Advocacy	Dependability	Imagination	Playfulness
Altruism	Determination	Independence	Positivity
Assertiveness	Dignity	Individuality	Proactivity
Autonomy	Drive	Innovation	Punctuality
Balance	Education	Integrity	Purpose
Belonging	Empathy	Intelligence	Reliability
Being the Best	Encouragement	Intuition	Respect
Boldness	Ethics	Joy	Responsibility
Calmness	Equality	Justice	Security
Challenge	Excellence	Kindness	Sensitivity
Charity	Excitement	Knowledge	Spirituality
Commitment	Exploration	Logic	Success
Community	Family	Loyalty	Teamwork
Collaboration	Freedom	Love	Thoughtfulness
Compassion	Friendship	Meticulousness	Tolerance
Creativity	Fun	Mindfulness	Vision
Credibility	Generosity	Moderation	Wealth
Competition	Goal Focused	Motivation	Wisdom

2. Now place similar values into five categories that make sense to you. Example:

Active	Caring	Love	Achievement	Intuition
Balance	Family	Loyalty	Being the Best	Personal
Health	Friendship	Teamwork	Creativity	Development
Knowledge	Happiness	Empathy	Drive	Spirituality
Mindfulness	Humour	Security	Encourag-	
Moderation	Loyalty		ement	
	Playfulness		Freedom	
			Imagination	
			Kindness	
			Purpose	

The following activity was adapted with permission from Taproot www.taproot.com

Your Values:

_____

_____

_____

_____

3. Select the word that best represents the whole of each group and underline it. These are your core values.

Active	Caring	<u>Love</u>	Achievement	Intuition
Balance	<u>Family</u>	Loyalty	Being the Best	Personal
<u>Health</u>	Friendship	Teamwork	Creativity	Development
Knowledge	Happiness	Empathy	Drive	<u>Spirituality</u>
Mindfulness	Humour	Security	Encourag-	
Moderation	Loyalty		ement	
	Playfulness		Freedom	
			Imagination	
			Kindness	
			<u>Purpose</u>	

4. Is over drinking effecting your ability to live in accordance with any of your personal values. If so, how?

_____

_____

Now it's time to think about how you can live in more alignment with your values in the future.

Some of your goals and actions may relate to changing your relationship with alcohol and others may relate to other aspects of your life. Its good to have a mix of both.

1. Take each of your core values and place them in the left-hand column as per the example on the next page.
2. In the central box give a description of what that value means to you (for example, to be a caring partner (Love) and any goals in relation to that value (for example, to be more thoughtful towards my partner and spend more time together).
3. In the third box, identify concrete actions you can take in the next month in support of your goals.

Value	Brief description of values and your related goals	How can I live a more values driven life? What action/s can I take in the next month?
Family	To be the best mum and daughter I can be. I want my family to feel proud of me. I want to rebuild and maintain good relationships with family members. I want to be fully present with my family and enjoy get togethers/parties/meals out with my mum and brothers without the overuse of alcohol getting in the way of spending meaningful time with them.	Spend more time with my mum and organise a lunch out for her upcoming birthday. Focus on cutting down on my drinking to healthier levels by planning ahead, using my moderation strategies such as tracking what I'm drinking, interspersing alcoholic and non alcoholic drinks.
Health	I want to achieve and maintain balance in all areas of my life and be moderate in my approach to exercise and food.	Plan and shop for some healthy meals at the weekend for the week ahead. Join up with the local gym and commit to going two or three times a week.
Spirituality	I want to explore my spiritual side. I'm interested in the spiritual realm.	Continue reading my spiritual books before bed and practice regular meditation once a day.
Purpose	I want to feel a sense of satisfaction in my job , to develop my skills and learn.	Choose and sign up for professional development course in the next month.
Love	I want to spend more time with my partner to enjoy and strengthen our relationship.	Book a babysitter and plan a date night a couple of times a month.

The following activity was adapted with permission from Taproot www.taproot.com

Your Turn

Value	Brief description of values and your related goals	How can I live a more values driven life? What action/s can I take in the next month?

The following activity was adapted with permission from Taproot www.taproot.com

Your Way Forward

Well done for taking the time to consider what is most important to you. This will help your moderation journey to flow much more easily. You will be able to refine your focus and start living in alignment with a deeper value-driven purpose rather than be swayed by shorter-term impulses. It is good to come back and complete this activity again every few months to review your progress and add new actions.

In addition, using your hypnotherapy recording provided will help you create space between stimulus and response, as well as to focus on the positive future you desire, which is in alignment with your core values. It is in that space where you can grow and develop.

Please go to the webpage www.drinklesslivewell.com to access the hypnosis recording that compliments this chapter entitled; **Tuning in with Your Values.**

PART TWO

Master Your Moderation Skills

Chapter 4

STEP FOUR:
IDENTIFY AND DEAL WITH YOUR
OVERDRINKING TRIGGERS

"To know thyself is the beginning of wisdom."

Socrates

Maybe, you have recognised scenarios where you tend to drink more heavily and others where you often drink more moderately. Triggers are social, environmental, or emotional situations that remind us of past alcohol use. In this chapter you will have the opportunity to clearly identify your unique trigger situations and choose healthier strategies for the future. The circumstances in which we drink will affect the way we drink. These factors can include: the people you are with; the place where you are drinking; the time of day or particular day of the week; hunger and thirst; how much money or alcohol is available; how you are feeling and what you are doing besides drinking.

Heavier drinking situations may also correspond with dealing with negative emotions, coping with stressful situations, simply drinking for pleasure or any combination of these. Examples of coping situations might be after a stressful day at work; the death of a loved one; a breakup; or a job loss. Everyone has challenging experiences in their life. Yet, people with alcohol issues tend to respond by overdrinking.

CLAIRE, 35, MANAGED HER EMOTIONAL AND CONTEXTUAL TRIGGERS TO MINIMISE OVERDRINKING

It is 6.30pm on a Friday evening and Claire has finished a week at the firm of accountants she works for in the city. Her friend Emma calls and suggests they have drinks in their local pub. Claire is tired, hungry, and frustrated, but she feels like a drink because she has been busy all week and wants to let off steam. She has also recently split up with her boyfriend and now lives alone, and she has no plans for the weekend ahead. Emma is there first and orders a bottle of wine, Emma is a fast drinker and tops up their drinks frequently. Other people in the pub are drinking heavily and there is loud music playing in the bar, which is darkly lit. Claire is not in a good situation right now. There are several aspects of this scenario that make it likely that Claire will drink too much. She is tired and hungry and she is still feeling emotionally vulnerable from the breakup with her boyfriend. As Claire embarked on her moderation journey, she gave careful thought to her particular triggers. She found that Friday nights were a danger point for her particularly when she was feeling stressed. She decided to plan something else on a Friday evening such as a gym class followed by a trip to the sauna and spa. She also made plans to catch up with Emma for coffee and brunch on the Saturday morning instead.

Furthermore, when Claire reflected on her moderate drinking situations, she realised that if she was at home relaxing with a nice meal, she could easily moderate her consumption and was happy to have a couple of glasses of wine and leave it at that. On Saturday evening, she enjoyed a half bottle of red while preparing and eating her spaghetti bolognese and then relaxed in front of the television. Consequently, Claire appreciated her weekend a great deal more without a hangover and felt very proud that she had made progress towards a healthier lifestyle.

Identify Your Overdrinking Triggers Exercise

In this exercise you can reflect on your life to help identify your past triggers for overdrinking which is a good indicator of scenarios in which we may face challenges in the future. The good news is that when we understand the circumstances where we are likely to overindulge, we have a choice to respond in healthier ways.

Each category allows you to consider a different part of your experience. In each of the following sections, think about instances where you overdrank and note down the details below.

IDENTIFY YOUR OVERDRINKING TRIGGERS EXERCISE

In this exercise you can reflect on your life to help identify your triggers for overdrinking. Each category allows you to consider a different part of your experience. In each of the following sections, think about instances where you overdrank and note down the details below.

Locations ...

_____

_____

_____

Timing ...

_____

_____

_____

People Involved ...

_____

_____

_____

Your Physical State ...

Activities ...

Work Related Circumstances ...

Feelings ...

Major Life Events ...

SUMMARISE YOUR OVER DRINKING TRIGGERS

Write down a list of your most problematic situations below, go back and revisit the trigger situations for patterns in areas that seem to go together. An example might be, being with the family or a celebration event such as Christmas or birthdays. Write a brief summary of key factors that triggered your overdrinking episodes, like the examples listed below.

Mark, 45, typical triggers
- After a stressful week.
- When relaxing with my mates at the local pub.
- After arguing with my girlfriend.
- Any time when I am feeling really angry.

Amy, 38, typical triggers
- At parties to help me feel more energised and sociable.
- After a breakup.
- When I am feeling anxious.

My Triggers Exercise

- _____

- _____

- _____

- _____

Manage Your Over Drinking Triggers
Congratulations for identifying your circumstances that are likely to trigger overdrinking. Now, you can choose better responses for the future. Many people find that moderate drinking in a trigger situation can be very challenging, so here are your options.

1. Avoid alcohol in that scenario.

2. Employ extreme caution with alcohol and plan ahead with moderation strategies that you think will work for you.

3. Don't attend.

Frederick Rotgers, author of the influential book *Responsible Drinking,* suggests that repeatedly being in situations that have triggered your excess drinking in the past, and not drinking at all, is one very good way to break those habits. In the next section, we look further into specific triggers and how to deal with them to give you inspiration for your future plan.

People

Many people drink alcohol to feel more relaxed when they are with friends and we can all think of heavy-drinking companions who may influence us into following suit. In this way, drinking may go hand-in-hand with warmth and good cheer that can be hard to turn away from. Other people find that alcohol makes them feel more comfortable when they are meeting other people for the first time. Some situations lend themselves well to moderation while others do not. People who put pressure on other people to drink or initiate drinking contests are going to encourage overdrinking.

In other scenarios, the way you feel when you are with certain people may influence your drinking habits. First date nerves, for example, are a prime example of where concern about the impression you are making can impact the level of alcohol you consume. Other people find that some people in their life try to 'police' how much they drink and that can often cause them to rebel and want to drink more.

Often overdrinking is part of what you do with particular people or certain groups of friends. Perhaps, there is a history of heavy drinking from college or university that has become ingrained over time. It is much harder to nurse a single drink when people around you are laughing and appearing to be having fun getting drunk. Maybe, you simply tend to stay out later with certain friends.

The amount of alcohol consumed can be directly affected by what else you do when you are with certain people or groups. If the activity is not compatible with alcohol, such as going to the cinema or going cycling, then the nature of the event is less likely to be focussed on alcohol. Others find being around certain people may lead them to curb drinking to make a good impression. Examples might include being with older family members or senior managers at a work-related function.

What You Can Do When You Overdrink with Certain People

In the early stages of your moderation journey, it may be wise to take a holiday from heavier drinkers to give yourself the space and time to establish your priorities in relation to your wellbeing. It is worth considering the nature of the relationship and how you want your friendships to feature in your future. As Stanton Peele PhD, psychologist and author of *The Truth About Addiction and Recovery* highlights, "Shaping your social experiences can support or undermine any individual skills that you develop and this more than anything else, keeps addiction out of your life." It is a question therefore, of arranging your social life to support the behaviours you wish to follow. You have the power to analyse, select and influence the social groups you engage with from this point forward.

Many people find that as they cut down on alcohol their relationships with other people change too. Certain friendships can become stronger and others may not last, as you realise that they were relationships based on drinking and with little else in common. When you reduce your drinking, it can create a defensive reaction in other people because it causes them to question their own relationship with alcohol. It can be like holding a mirror up to their own behaviour. It is worth being aware of this because these can be challenging moments. However, you will find a way around this situation and listed below are several suggestions for your consideration.

1. If the people you hang around with are likely to push drinks, you can strengthen your ability to refuse by rehearsing a response. Humour is a positive strategy that can put other people at ease. You should use a one liner that you feel most happy with. It is a good idea to choose someone you trust to rehearse it with, so you become comfortable before you arrive at your destination. When you are relaxed and confident, other people around you will react positively.

Here are examples of statements that other people have found useful.
- I am doing a cleanse.
- I am on antibiotics.
- I am doing dry January/November, or whatever month you are in.
- I have an early meeting/exercise class booked.
- No, I am not pregnant, I simply feel like drinking water.
- I am giving up alcohol for Lent.

- Cutting down on drinking is my New Year's resolution.
- My doctor wants me to lose a few pounds.
- I am watching my sugar level.

2. Suggest meeting them at places other than where you might ordinarily drink. Why not meet for coffee or brunch instead? This way, you are communicating that you value the relationship but do not want to hang out somewhere you will be tempted to drink.

3. Ask for support. This will involve telling your friends that you are focussing on moderating your drinking and asking them to assist you. You may wish to let them know that you are not asking them to change but you feel it is time for you to cut down and would appreciate their help. Be specific about what is or isn't helpful to you.

CHRIS, 34, SHARED HIS MODERATION GOAL FOR SUCCESS

Chris found that bringing his friend on board with his plan for change really helped him achieve his moderation goals. Chris had a responsible job and he wanted to escape the pressures of work at the end of a busy week. His old university friend Alistair lived nearby and they went out together most Friday nights. Alistair was also a heavy drinker and liked to buy rounds for them both. They often met after work and stayed out all night. Chris enjoyed hanging out with his old friend and talking about university times, but he found that the hangovers were getting worse and he was taking a whole weekend to recover. He also felt a lot of anxiety and self-loathing the day after drinking and realised things had to change. Chris talked with Alistair about why and how he wanted to reduce his drinking and suggested they shared other activities that did not involve alcohol. To his surprise Alistair wanted to cut down too. They decided they would like to play more sports and joined a local volleyball club, which was a fun way to meet other people in the neighborhood. When they went out in the evening they often went for a meal or to the cinema where the main focus was not on drinking. They did go out periodically to the pub for special occasions with other friends who lived in the area. However, on these occasions Chris was a great deal more mindful of his alcohol consumption. He used moderation strategies such as interspersing alcoholic beverages with non-alcoholic drinks. In addition, he made plans the next day and thought forward to how he wanted to feel in the morning. Chris managed to cut down the instances of overdrinking dramatically and saw improvements in his sleep and mood, which inspired him to continue developing his self-knowledge and moderation skills.

Drinking Alone

Another classic situation for overdrinking is being alone. When socialising with others many people are concerned with the impression they are making, which deters them from overdrinking. Yet when we are alone, the social controls are off and temptation can increase. A helpful strategy to counter the tendency to overdrink is to change the setting in which you consume alcohol. You could change the seat in which you sit, or perhaps the room, or the glass that you use to shake up the habit.

It is also important to figure out the reason for the overdrinking because there is likely to be an underlying emotional trigger, such as loneliness, or boredom. It can be helpful to conduct an assessment of your moods when you are alone.

An essential part of moderation is tracking what you drink on a daily or weekly basis. At the point of recording how much alcohol you have consumed you can also note down your mood and the particular circumstances of the day. You can look for patterns, such as whether a particular emotion led to overdrinking.

When you have more of a handle of how your emotions affect your drinking, you will be better equipped to deal with the situation. You may wish to brainstorm pleasurable, emotionally supportive, or stimulating activities you can engage in as a counter to any desire to overdrink. You may eventually conclude from your observations that there are certain mood states when alcohol is best avoided, and self-care is what is needed to restore your emotional equilibrium.

Cope With Negative Emotions

As you reflect on your relationship with alcohol, it may become apparent that you use it as a way to control your feelings. It may also be an attempt to shield yourself from your emotions in relation to your life experiences. Furthermore, interpersonal relationships, as well as world events can trigger the overconsumption of alcohol for people with alcohol issues. The Global Drugs Survey in 2020 highlighted that 48 per cent of Britons consumed more alcohol because of anxiety, depression and loneliness during the Covid-19 pandemic.

Alcohol can provide temporary relief from negative emotions and allow people to forget about their problems for a short while. However, heavy drinking can complicate such feelings and worsen them because they are compounded with alcohol-related issues. Research by Drinkaware UK states that regular alcohol use interrupts the neurotransmitters that are required for the regulation of our moods. It also narrows our perception, so we are less effective at responding to cues in our immediate environment. People often report that when they use alcohol to alter their mood, they often feel even worse for several days afterwards. Cyndi Turner, author of *The Clinician's Guide to Alcohol Moderation* points out that, "When a substance gives an emotional lift, there will be a converse reaction with an even worse mood as a result. In the long run, people find themselves on a never-ending cycle where they are trying to recover from the last emotional dip."

Taking charge of your life involves an acceptance of your thoughts, feelings and experiences. If you dull or block out your responses to life, you never get the opportunity to learn how to tolerate and cope with difficult emotions. It is much healthier to experience the flow of your feelings and let them pass naturally. Furthermore, it is much easier to make changes to enhance your moods and quality of life when you have a good level of knowledge relating to your emotional responses and needs. This may be challenging at first and many people report feeling a little bit 'raw' at the start of the moderation journey. However, it becomes easier over time and you will find that as you settle into moderate drinking your moods will likely be greatly improved. Many people report enjoying better sleep; having more energy; and an increased ability to think and act clearly in stressful situations. Others notice that life seems to flow more easily and they are more motivated and productive in all areas of their life.

Stress

Negative emotions commonly involve the feeling of being overburdened. Whether stress originates from your personal or professional life, the first stage of improving your mood is pinpointing the cause. You may wish to employ a brainstorming technique to generate multiple ideas for dealing with the issue constructively. Taking control of the situation is empowering and honing your problem-solving skills will serve you well for the future.

Stress Busting Ideas

1. Get moving; regular exercise is a brilliant medicine for feeling calmer. It will not eradicate stress completely, but it will reduce the emotional intensity of your thoughts and help clear your mind.
2. Connect with other people; a strong support system of family, friends and colleagues can provide comfort in challenging times. It is always worth investing in your relationships. Spending time with friends also helps you to relax and see life from a different perspective.

3. Make sure you have regular breaks during your working day and when you take lunch leave your desk and have some fresh air if possible.

4. Deep Breathing Exercise; the following exercise will put you in a state of comfortable relaxation. It will be most effective if it is part of your daily routine. It only takes a few minutes and can be conducted anywhere.

- Sit on a supportive chair, lie on a bed, or a yoga mat on the floor.
- Make yourself as comfortable as you can, by loosening any clothes that feel restrictive.
- If you are sitting, put your feet flat on the floor.
- Breath in through your nose and out through your mouth gently, smoothly and regularly.
- You may find it helpful to count in for five and out for five.
- Continue this for three to five minutes.

Anger

Frustration and anger are two of the most common negative feeling states and there are many good books written about this subject. One way of managing anger is noticing when it is building up and seeing if you can stay calm under pressure. An anger diary may be helpful in allowing you to build up your self-knowledge of your triggers.

Assertive communication can help prevent the build-up of negative emotions and help you relate to other people more effectively. Being assertive involves getting your point across in a firm manner without being aggressive. It is important to balance your needs against the needs of other people.

This is a list of tips for assertive communication.

- Listen carefully to what other people have to say.
- Think about what you mean to say before saying it and think about what other people may take from what you say.
- No one can argue with how a particular behaviour makes you feel. Use statements such as when you do X it makes me feel like Y.
- Try to be as clear as possible and express yourself in a considered way.
- Avoid using an angry tone or confrontational style.

Anxiety

Anxiety can be a condition requiring medical treatment or in other cases it can be a milder issue that many people experience from time-to-time. Drinking alcohol may relieve anxiety temporarily. However, these effects diminish fast and relying on alcohol to mask anxiety can build up a reliance on it to unwind. Over time you can create a tolerance to alcohol meaning that you need to drink more alcohol to achieve the same feeling. When alcohol is overused, anxiety and panic can rebound with a greater severity and lead to a spiral of further drinking. If anxiety has been a significant feature of your life for some time, professional assistance can help. A doctor may recommend cognitive behavioural therapy, counselling, and in some cases, medication alongside therapy.

MARIA, 27, ADDRESSED HER ANXIETY TRIGGERS TO STRENGTHEN HER MODERATION GOALS

Maria had been anxious since her late teens but her stressful job as a teacher in her twenties really ramped up her anxiety. Even at weekends she was constantly thinking about her work and worrying that she had not done a good enough job. These thoughts went around and around in her head and she couldn't switch off. After a busy day's teaching and with the frequent observations of her work, Maria turned to wine after work in the evening and at weekends. A couple of glasses helped her to calm down and slow her busy mind. Over time she saw her consumption rise and she started to drink up to a bottle of wine every night. She often woke up in the early hours feeling sweaty and panicky, unable to go back to sleep. She stared at the wall and only worried more. It was a vicious circle; anxiety made her drink, and she was drinking to quell the ensuing feelings of panic. Maria knew this self-medication was getting worse and she sought professional help. With support, Maria took three months off alcohol, to deal with the underlying issues. Through her doctor she was referred to a cognitive behavioural therapist who helped her greatly reduce and manage her anxiety. She also created a drinking moderation plan and she slowly reintroduced alcohol and was able to moderate her intake successfully and feel a great deal better.

Depression

Many of us have days when we feel low. However, for some people such feelings don't go away, they may worsen and affect everyday life. Depression involves sadness, a lack of motivation and energy, boredom and low self-esteem, along with a lack of enjoyment or interest in things that previously made you happy. If feelings last consistently for more than two weeks or become incapacitating, or if you have suicidal or intrusive thoughts, you should speak with your doctor. For people whose depression affects their ability to function on a daily basis, a doctor may recommend cognitive behavioural therapy, counselling, and in some cases, medication alongside therapy. For people with drinking issues, depression can be the cause or the result of heavy alcohol use. Research compiled by Drinkaware about alcohol and mental health states that alcohol is known to affect multiple nerve-chemical systems, which are important in regulating our emotions and drinking heavily can lead to a low mood.

Additional Triggers

There can be other factors, which affect the way we drink and they will be unique to everyone. This is a list of examples.

- Hearing a particular piece of music.
- Feeling a lack of creativity.
- Being told that you cannot have something.
- Being rejected.
- Feeling lonely.
- Alcohol adverts on television.

Alcohol, beer especially, can often be advertised as a thirst-quenching beverage. However, ideas about alcohol being a good refresher are the product of advertising, social learning and imagination. It is not a good idea to drink alcohol when you are thirsty because alcohol will dehydrate you further. There is nothing better to satisfy your thirst than water. When you decide to drink however, make sure you are hydrated before you have an alcoholic beverage and intersperse water with your alcoholic drinks.

Hunger can be a trigger for many people to overdrink. Alcohol can give us a small spurt of energy in the form of empty calories. As you continue to drink alcohol it can actually diminish your appetite, leaving you drinking instead of eating healthy food. It is wise not to drink on an empty stomach because the alcohol will have a stronger effect on the body and mind.

Manage Your Overdrinking Triggers

In the examples below you can see how a range of overdrinking trigger situations have been coped with positively.

JOHN, 47, CREATED HIS OVERDRINKING TRIGGER MANAGEMENT PLAN

My Overdrinking Trigger

After work drinks with the heavy-drinking office crowd, at the end of a busy and stressful week.

My Management

Give an excuse to the office crowd. Make plans for dinner and go to see a movie with good friend Mark who is a moderate drinker.

My Overdrinking Trigger

Family birthday party with copious amounts of alcohol available over a long period.

My Management

Skip the alcohol, have soft drinks and enjoy the nice food. Will drive to the party and offer lifts to other family members. Book an early exercise class the next day.

MY OVERDRINKING TRIGGER MANAGEMENT PLAN EXERCISE

Below is a space for you to make notes about how you can manage your key trigger scenarios in the future.

My Overdrinking Trigger

My Management

My Overdrinking Trigger

My Management

My Overdrinking Trigger

_____

_____

My Management

_____

_____

My Overdrinking Trigger

_____

_____

My Management

_____

_____

_____

Moderate Drinking Situations

Exactly as some circumstances lend themselves to overdrinking, there may be other occasions that are conducive to moderate drinking, which can show you that you have the ability to moderate successfully. Generally speaking, those people who are not heavy drinkers themselves will make it easier for you to drink moderately. You will do well to spend more time with these people and gain their support. Perhaps, it is time to consider friendships that you may have neglected for a while or try a new friendship group where there is no shared overdrinking history.

Firstly, list your examples below and secondly, ask yourself the following questions about these situations.

1. My moderate drinking situations

2. Why do these circumstances lend themselves to moderation?

3. What I do to moderate

Your Way Forward

At this point, you will be developing a good understanding of your unique triggers that led you to overdrinking in the past. This knowledge facilitates powerful choices for you to take a different course of action and create an improved relationship with alcohol and with yourself.

In addition, understanding where you tend to drink moderately illustrates the type of situations that it is safest for you to drink and showcases your current moderate drinking skills. Many people find as they progress on their journey that social situations are greatly improved by drinking moderately, and in many cases not drinking at all.

The wonderful news is that over time you will create distance from the unwanted behaviours and feel stronger and more confident as the healthier responses become second nature.

Chapter 5

STEP FIVE:
SET YOUR LIMITS AND
MODERATION TOOLS

*"The goal is not to be better than the other man,
but your previous self."*

Dalai Lama

To master any skill and achieve lasting change, there are two key elements. Firstly, a clear objective and secondly, accurate feedback about how you are getting on. Setting limits for yourself is often the first measure people attempt when cutting down on drinking and it is perhaps the most straightforward action. Collecting data is a primary aspect of any behaviour change journey, and in the first part of this chapter, you will learn how to set healthy limits and monitor your progress along the way. Many people find that the data forms an extremely rewarding and concrete source of information towards the acquisition and maintenance of a healthy lifestyle. The second part of this chapter includes general moderation tools that other people have found helpful.

How Much Is Enough?

Perhaps the most crucial aspect that determines success with alcohol moderation is a real commitment to the awareness that the benefits of drinking alcohol come from consuming a small number of drinks. According to Rotgers' book *Responsible Drinking* it is not necessary to come to the realisation that 'less is more' straightaway. However, keep it in consideration as a commitment that you would like to arrive at through your own experience because this is the true essence of moderation.

STEWART, 54, DESCRIBED THE BENEFITS OF MODERATION
"The good aspects always occur during the first two or three small beers. I have a nice relaxed fuzzy feeling and I really enjoy the taste. If I drink more than three, the negatives creep

in and I find that I do not sleep as well and I feel under par the next day. This understanding helps to motivate and remind me to stick to my limit and I now enjoy savouring my drink instead of downing it mindlessly."

The precise number of 'good ones' will be different for each individual. However, it will consistently be a small number of drinks, most likely one, two or three. Many people report that when they cut down on alcohol their tolerance is lowered so they actually need to drink less to achieve the positive relaxing effects of the alcohol. The wonderful news is that when your system has recalibrated in this way you can enjoy the positives without the negative aspects.

Set Your Limits

Current guidelines in the UK as stated by the chief medical officer detail that for both men and women to keep health risks from alcohol to a low level it is safest not to drink more than fourteen units per week on a regular basis. Furthermore, if you drink regularly as much as fourteen units per week you should spread them across three or more days. The Drink Aware website states that an example of low-risk drinking is a limit of six medium glasses of wine (175ml at 13.5 per cent) or six pints of beer (4 per cent) per week.

According to the dietary guidelines for Americans, drinking moderately is defined as two standard drinks or less per day for men or one standard drink or less in a day for women. A standard drink is defined as 12oz of beer at 5% abv, 8oz of malt liquor at 7% abv, 5oz of wine at 12% abv or 1.5oz of distilled spirits at 40% (80 proof) abv.

It is useful that most alcoholic beverages now come with the units or number of standard drinks labelled on the product. There are also many handy online calculators and apps to quickly calculate how many units are in different combinations of strength and size of drinks. Two of my current favourites are the unit calculator on Alcoholchange.org and the Drinkaware app, which you can download to a smartphone. With these limits in mind, you might like to think about how you are going to spread your allocation through the week. You might decide to have four alcohol free days and three days where you consume alcohol. You will be able to record your limits in the moderation plan below. For example, "On the three days that I drink I will have no more than four and a half units (or one or two standard drinks in the case of US moderators)." This will keep you comfortably within the healthy range. Work out what you would like to drink and then you can plan ahead.

Develop an Alcohol Moderation Action Plan Exercise

Your Alcohol Moderation Action Plan is a set of guidelines around your intended future drinking behaviour. This is a great time to start thinking about what kind of drinker you want to be and work backwards from there. Your action plan is a working document that can be amended as you progress along your moderation journey. Some people find, for example, that previously undiscovered triggers may arise and cause a lapse. You can change your action plan accordingly, highlighting times when it is safest not to drink.

Your first plan is a starting point to see what is possible and desirable in terms of your drinking behaviour. It's important to take a flexible approach to your guidelines and review your action plan every few months to see how the types and amounts of alcohol are affecting your mind and body and change them as appropriate.

Below is a list of the different aspects of the plan for your consideration.

Think carefully about, and write down, the key benefits of cutting down and how this will improve your life, now and in the future because this will really supercharge your motivation levels.

When is it safest not to drink?
Consider the trigger points at which you are likely to overdrink, this may include: particular places; events; emotional states; times; or people you are with. It will most likely correlate to occasions when you have drunk too much in the past.

Consider the period in which you drink
Given that the amounts of alcohol classed as healthy are pretty low, you are wise to limit a drinking session to the times when you can savour and enjoy it in a mindful way. A majority of people's action plans will specify that they will only drink when they are at the event, restaurant, wedding, dinner party etc. For example, if you are having alcohol at home, you might plan only to drink after six o'clock, perhaps one drink before dinner and one during the meal. Think carefully about what will work for you.

How many units is right for you?

You have read about the recommended healthy guidelines in the earlier section. However, it is essential to be in tune with the effects on your body to discover your 'sweet spot'. This is the level where you can have the relaxing effects of alcohol but when it does not affect your self-control. Men can drink more alcohol than women with fewer effects. Some people report that when they go over a certain number of units or standard drinks, they find it more challenging to stay within their limits. It is also worth noting that if you have gone through a period of abstinence, your tolerance will have decreased, and you will be affected by smaller amounts of alcohol. Think carefully about what will work for you and write it down.

Alcohol free time

Alcohol-free days are one of your most important tools in the moderation process. It is a good idea to plan enjoyable and relaxing activities on these days, especially if this is a new regime for you. It might be a long bubble bath, cooking a nice dinner, or a film night. The benefits of alcohol-free days are compelling because you will create a space unclouded by alcohol to develop your resolution for a brand-new lifestyle. Also, you will clarify your drinking ground rules and control strategies, as well as lowering your weekly consumption with ease. Furthermore, you start to tune into the positive experiences in life that don't involve alcohol to further strengthen your resolve.

TONY, 46, SHARED HIS ALCOHOL MODERATION ACTION PLAN

<u>I embrace alcohol moderation because ...</u>

I want to be a good father to my kids and husband to my wife, to be present, have energy and to always be reliable and consistent.

I want to have energy to cycle and play football, to stay in shape and feel healthy.

I want to be focussed and productive at work, to progress in my career and gain promotion.

<u>It is safest not to drink in these circumstances ...</u>

When I have had an argument with my wife.

When I haven't eaten.

When I am at a long drinking event, such as a wedding.

<u>I will only drink during the period of ...</u>

After 6pm and until I have finished the evening meal.

**<u>I will have no more than... units/standard drinks on .....
days per week...</u>**

I will have no more than four units on three days per week.

<u>I will have ..... alcohol-free days per week.</u>

I will have four alcohol-free days per week.

ALCOHOL MODERATION ACTION PLAN

For you to fill in for yourself, print and refer to daily to keep you on track.

I embrace alcohol moderation because; ...

It is safest not to drink in these circumstances; ...

I will only drink during the period of; ...

I will have no more than ... units/standard drinks on ... days per week.

I will have ... alcohol-free days per week.

With kind permission of Cyndi Turner, LCSW, LSATP, MAC, adapted from *Practicing Alcohol Moderation: A Comprehensive Workbook.*

Keep Track of Your Drinks

Many people find it useful to download an app to their phone or use a spreadsheet on the computer, whereas other people prefer to use a small diary. Keeping good records of your alcohol use is far better than occasionally thinking about how you have done. Over a longer period, you may also like to record the information on a wall planner or calendar. Psychologists call this technique 'self-monitoring' and there are four compelling reasons why it will supercharge your moderation journey.

1. Of primary importance is accurate feedback about how you are getting on. When you count your drinks, the figures do not lie. You will know for sure that you are making progress in a positive direction. Either you are moving towards your goal or you are not.

2. Self-monitoring automatically helps you reduce your drinking because you are giving it your focus and making it a daily or weekly priority. Also, you are setting a personal intention for yourself and your self-care, which is a powerful way to achieve goals. When I ask people about moderation techniques that they find most useful, the element that was often cited was keeping records.

3. Monitoring your alcohol intake over time leads to increased self-knowledge concerning your drinking patterns. You may discover times when you overdrink that shed light on perhaps a previously undiscovered trigger.

4. Self-monitoring can be very motivating because you can see positive changes over time. If you have a slip, it can be useful to see how far you have come and it helps to put the lapse in perspective.

JOANNA, 38, SET HER LIMITS AND RECORDED HER INTAKE

Joanna was a doctor with a stressful job at a busy medical practice. At university she had enjoyed drinking socially with friends. As she progressed in her career, she found she often drank after work to relieve stress and calm her busy mind. A couple of large glasses every night, plus more at the weekend was pushing her intake up to an average of four or five bottles of wine per week. She was starting to feel sluggish in the mornings and was putting on weight. Her low energy levels meant that she didn't feel like exercising and looking after herself, which further compounded the issue.

Her husband was starting to express concern about her drinking, and it was this that first inspired Joanna to change her drinking habits, along with her growing realisation that alcohol was playing an increasingly unhealthy role in her life. Joanna found that setting limits and tracking her units in a small diary helped her to be more mindful of what and when she was drinking. She set her target at three days where she allowed herself between four to five units and four alcohol-free days per week. She liked to drink sparkling wine and she discovered that her supermarket stocked mini (200ml) bottles of prosecco. On her allocated drinking days, she allowed herself two mini bottles and enjoyed them while preparing and during her evening meal.

In the past, after opening a bottle she was tempted to finish it on her own because her husband did not drink wine. With the mini bottles, she found it easier to stay within limits by having less alcohol available. The end of the meal signified the 'full stop' to her drinking and she found also that once she had consumed a satisfying meal, she no longer wanted any more alcohol.

Joanna found that she was looking after her overall health much more effectively as she cut down on her drinking. She returned to running three times a week which helped with her stress levels. As well as exercising, she found that listening to a short hypnotherapy meditation audio when she arrived home from work allowed her to unwind from the working day.

Joanna had set a clear goal and kept accurate records to show her steps towards healthier drinking patterns. As her moderation journey progressed, she slept better, had more energy and felt calmer generally. Joanna also felt more connected in her relationships, especially with her husband.

Additional Moderation Tools

This section gives you a selection of further moderation tools to help you stay on track.

Limit availability

This technique is most applicable if you drink at home. Only keep small amounts of alcohol in the house or buy on the day what you plan to consume. It can be tempting to finish a bottle of wine once opened, so why not purchase smaller bottles of wine to help keep you on track.

Drink from a smaller glass

Choosing a dainty glass and sip slowly is a technique that works well for many of my clients.

Reward your success

It is important to reward yourself along the way to keep up your motivation. Even if your progress has been small, give yourself some praise.

EMILY, 36, PLANNED A SPECIAL REWARD, WHICH MOTIVATED HER MODERATION JOURNEY

Emily worked out the cost of her pampering facial and broke it down into smaller chunks. Each time she successfully navigated a social event without overdrinking, she transferred money into a dormant instant access account. She had a banking app on her phone, and she liked to see the figure mounting up each time she had moderation success. When she had saved enough money she treated herself to the facial treatment, which she really appreciated. She said that it felt great to have something enjoyable to look forward to that was a tangible measure of her progress.

Take a few minutes to think about some gratifying rewards, such as a trip away or an experience that you enjoy. It might be a: massage; special takeaway; new clothes; or perhaps some jewellery you have been coveting.

What are the rewards perfectly suited to you? Record your ideas below.

1.

_____

_____

2.

_____

_____

3.

_____

_____

Positive self-talk

How we talk to ourselves is important, especially when we are changing our behaviour. We have to become our own best friend and give ourselves a boost, particularly when we are navigating the early stages of moderation, which can be daunting. All changes can be anxiety inducing, but the trick is to push through and keep going because it will become easier over time as new behaviours become established. Having a positive internal dialogue helps you to stay upbeat and confident. Here are some examples for inspiration.

"I'm going to have a good time tonight and really look after myself."

"I'm really proud of how far I have come on this moderation journey."

"Socialising without alcohol is going to become easier and easier, it simply takes practice."

"Everyone has the right to improve their life and that includes me."

What might you say to yourself?

Record below at least four statements that express something favourable about you and your future plans.

1.

2.

3.

4.

Quench your thirst

On many occasions a strong urge for alcohol simply can be a natural thirst for water. When entering a drinking situation make sure you are hydrated or have a non-alcoholic drink when you first arrive.

Bring your own alternatives

There are so many great options on the market now, such as 0.5 per cent beers, ciders or wines that look and taste very similar to full-strength beverages. Or you may prefer a fruit juice or soft drink. Many people find that taking a selection of their own no- or low-alcoholic drinks is a great way to prepare.

> **ANDREW, 29, WAS EMPOWERED BY TAKING CONTROL AND PLANNING AHEAD**
>
> "Friends of mine had decided to meet in the park for a few drinks on bank holiday because the weather was warm. I was new to moderation and didn't feel like announcing that I was cutting back. Group social events had been a trigger for overindulging in the past and I knew it was safest not to drink. Instead of joining in with the prosecco, I took a few cold very low-alcohol ciders along. No one even batted an eyelid that I wasn't joining in with the wine and I had a nice afternoon catching up with friends. I didn't feel deprived because I had my own stash of nice drinks and a few snacks to hand around to other people too. It was a great feeling to wake up on Sunday morning feeling fresh and happy and to know that I had stuck to my plan. Another social event successfully navigated!"

Eat

Having something to eat before or with alcoholic drinks slows down the rate at which alcohol gets into your bloodstream and takes effect on your mind and body. If we drink on an empty stomach the effect can come as a surprise and take us off guard before we can fully appreciate what is happening.

Delay or leave early

Delaying your first alcoholic drink can be a simple and effective tool for staying within your limits. This may involve arriving at an event later or leaving early, especially if the gathering is getting a bit booze heavy for you to moderate with ease. If you find your resolve slipping, take yourself off for a relaxing night's sleep and think how good you will feel in the morning.

Slow down

Another drinking control technique involves training yourself to sip your drink rather than gulp it down mindlessly. Learning to take sips and spacing them out can be an excellent way to slow down your intake of alcohol. Another good tip for slowing down is to put your glass down between sips.

Listen to hypnotherapy recordings before an event

Your hypnotherapy recordings are designed to be motivating, as well as deeply implanting beneficial suggestions into your unconscious mind. Before you attend a party or social gathering, why not choose a recording to help you relax beforehand whilst focussing on the positive benefits of sticking to your moderation plan. Find a nice quiet place to relax and get yourself comfortable as you listen to your chosen track. By the time the event comes around, you will be feeling ready to have a great time without overdrinking.

Keep tomorrow in mind

It can be useful when you are planning to consume alcohol to think about tomorrow or 'playing it forward'. We can become stuck in short-term thinking and focusing on 'the now' which can often lead to overdrinking. As an alternative, think about your responsibilities and goals when the idea of 'just one more for the road' pops into your head. It can also be powerful to focus on how positive you will feel in the morning, if you take good care of yourself and stay within your limits.

HANNAH, 32, CHOSE A POSITIVE PATH

Hannah had been on her moderation journey for about six months and had a pretty good understanding of what her overdrinking triggers were. A danger point for her was when she got together with her old friend Amy who she had been drinking with since they left secondary school. Amy could polish a bottle of wine off in record time and often set a quick pace when it came to their meetups.

Hannah was looking forward to Amy coming over on a Friday evening for a catch up and takeaway, but she thought if she started drinking she was likely to get carried away. Hannah decided it was best to avoid alcohol and she found it helpful to play the situation forward in her mind. If she were to drink as she had done in the past it was highly probable that she would end up getting through two bottles of wine, staying up late, smoking cigarettes, having an awful sleep, feeling terrible the next day and end up missing her exercise class. Just the thought of all those negative consequences made Hannah cringe, yet it really strengthened her resolve. After this, in contrast she thought about how nice she would feel after a refreshing night's sleep, a lovely cup of tea in bed, knowing that she had really looked after herself. Hannah also planned to deposit the money she would have spent on wine towards some special new clothes as her motivational reward. This would give her a real sense of satisfaction that she had stuck to her intentions and was making good progress.

Enjoy the event

When you embark on a new moderation journey it's beneficial to pay close attention to what you are doing when you are drinking. The essence of moderation is to see alcohol as a small enjoyable part of the occasion, but not the sole source of pleasure. It can be useful to focus on what else you appreciate during the event, perhaps the music, the setting, the food, or the interaction with other people.

ALAN, 62, INCREASED HIS SELF-CARE THROUGH PLANNING

When Alan went out for dinner with his friends, he was aware that he often overdrank and felt awful the next day. He found that his excitement leading up to seeing his friends meant that felt he had to have a couple of drinks to calm his nerves, which led to a few more after that. When he began his moderation journey, he knew that he had to try a different approach. He still felt excited before a get-together, but he tried to accept his feelings instead of masking them with alcohol. He also allowed himself more time to get ready and arrive early at the restaurant so he could consciously relax beforehand. During the meal he chose to drink low-alcohol drinks and sip slowly. He found that after about half an hour into the event he felt a lot more at ease and enjoyed the company of his friends and tuned into the conversation with greater ease. Alan also noticed that by focussing on the food and the pleasant surroundings of the restaurant he found more to enjoy about the event. On mastering this approach, Alan felt a great sense of achievement and found his self-confidence increasing over time.

Deal with overdrinking urges

For many people there are instances after we have consumed a drink or two when our inner voice says, "Why not let your hair down?" and it attempts to derail our best laid plans for moderation. The first reason is that your blood alcohol level has risen to a point where your self-control and judgement become impaired and your plans can go astray. Another critical factor that may bring on overdrinking urges detailed in Rotgers' book Responsible Drinking is; "Drinking alcohol in circumstances that involve your overdrinking triggers." You may have made plans to avoid this, however these triggers can occasionally catch you unaware or you may not be familiar with all of them during your early efforts at moderation.

This does not mean that we are powerless over alcohol. However, we have taken enough of the drug to impede our higher thought centres. In this situation, we are much less likely to think of the long-term benefits of moderation and instead focus on our immediate gratification. In this irrational state you might not think of the emotional and physical pain of the hangover to come. You might notice that the urge accompanies a voice in your head that tells you that you can bend the rules a little on this occasion. You might be telling yourself things such as, "I deserve a good time because I have been working so hard at the moment" or "I don't have to get up early for anything tomorrow." It is a good idea to recognise the typical rebellious thoughts in that instance, so you can be aware of them and challenge them to bring rationality back to the situation. You can find strength in talking back to the wayward voices, for example, "I am sticking to my plan of three drinks," or "I want to feel good tomorrow."

Wait it out

The concept of Surfing the Urge was developed by the late Alan Marlett, professor of psychology at The Addictive Behaviour Research Centre at the University of Washington, US. He suggested that it is important to remember how all cravings pass if you accept them and ride them out; safe in the knowledge they will soon crest like a wave and pass, making you stronger for the future.

Special Ticket Events

While moderate drinking of 14 units spread approximately across three days per week is a healthy guideline most of the time, there may be infrequent positive social occasions when you decide to allow yourself to be a little more indulgent. Special Ticket Events must be undertaken with planning and care for obvious reasons, and I suggest that they are suitable when stable moderation has been achieved over a longer period. You must also consider if it is safe for you to do this, and some people decide for reasons of their own safety and sanity it is not appropriate. An example of a Special Ticket Event might be a wedding or special birthday party with friends. You may allow yourself perhaps only two or three Special Ticket Events per year. Some people find that they are helpful in letting them occasionally blow off some steam and help them to stay on track the rest of the year. You might create a detailed plan of how you will manage the event, the type and quantity of drinks you intend to consume, making sure you eat, are rested or other such techniques to ensure harm is minimised and an overall positive experience is achieved.

TAMMY, 41, PLANNED HER SPECIAL TICKET EVENT AND ENJOYED A RARE NIGHT OUT WITH COLLEAGUES

Tammy had been moderating successfully for a couple of years and found that her health, confidence and wellbeing had increased to a great extent. She had been invited to a reunion of the nurses she trained with in another city, and they had planned a big party with music and dancing. While Tammy was nervous about attending, she also really wanted to have a fun night out and felt she could plan to keep harm to a minimum. She organised with one of the other friends attending to go together, and she made sure she had eaten and was well rested before the event. It was on a weekend, so she didn't have to worry about work the next day. She also booked a hotel room and her husband was looking after their little girl for the weekend. Tammy had spoken with her therapist before the event and planned how it could be safely managed.

On the day of the event, Tammy took good care of herself and checked in with her husband and mum for emotional support. The evening went as planned, she enjoyed catching up with her friends and she and another mate went out dancing afterwards. She stayed out much later than she had planned, but she was never alone and was well supported. The next day she was very tired but emotionally felt okay. Although it was enjoyable, she realised it was not something she wanted to do on a regular basis because she much preferred her moderate lifestyle, however it was a good learning experience. Tammy also felt a sense of achievement that she had managed it safely.

Tammy's Example of a Planned Infrequent Special Ticket Event

1. **Describe the nature of the event;** reunion of nurse friends at a pub with night out in town planned afterwards.

2. **Are there any of your particular triggers or hazards present, if so, how will you manage these?** Excitement can be a trigger for overdrinking. I plan to have a calm week leading up to the event, exercise, and meditation to ensure emotional and mental equilibrium. My tiredness trigger; ensure that I have plenty of rest before the event. My hunger trigger; I will have a good meal before going out.

3. **What do you plan to drink and how much?** I plan to have a couple of drinks before I go out, drink slowly and mindfully at the event and hydrate myself with sparkling water throughout the evening, only one bottle of wine in total throughout the evening.

4. **What strategies will you put in place to help you stick to your plan?** Delaying starting drinking. Feeling safe and emotionally supported. Planning ahead so I feel organised, supported and happy about all aspects of the event.

5. **Reflection from this event; what did you learn?** I enjoyed the preparation for the event and the party itself, but I felt very tired the week afterwards and it cost quite a lot of money altogether. I much prefer moderate drinking and looking after myself so I can be healthy and productive. I am glad I went because I gained confidence from the achievement of generally managing it well. I also learned that it is easy to slip back into my 'party girl' ways but actually I much prefer my life now, as a healthy moderate drinker.

Plan Your Infrequent Special Ticket Event Exercise

1. Describe the nature of the event.

2. Are there any of your particular triggers present, if so, how will you manage these?

3. What do you plan to drink and how much?

4. What strategies will you put in place to help you stick to your plan?

_____

_____

5. Reflection from this event; what did you learn?

_____

_____

Your Way Forward

Congratulations! By now you have a good grasp of the healthy limits to aim for on your moderation journey. I hope you enjoy creating your plan and keeping notes of all you drink in your chosen format. Many people find that having an Alcohol Moderation Action Plan provides or restores structure to a life that was previously more chaotic. These parameters are an essential part of bringing a sense of equilibrium and highlighting progress towards enhanced physical and mental wellbeing.

The great news is that over time it will become natural to stay within your limits and enjoy the pleasant aspects of moderate drinking and move away from your overdrinking of the past. This is a new beginning for you to look forward to because we all have the right to move on in our lives and evolve positively.

Please go to the webpage www.drinklesslivewell.com to access the hypnosis recording that compliments this chapter entitled; *Mastering Moderation Skills.*

Chapter 6

STEP SIX:
TAKE BREAKS FROM ALCOHOL

*"What we achieve inwardly will change
outer reality."*

Otto Rank

Many people discover that a period of abstinence is fundamental in changing their drinking behaviours for the better. I recommend a month alcohol-free at the start of your moderation journey. This will allow you to break old unwanted habits and to form new beneficial ways of coping with, and enjoying life, without booze as a central aspect. Many people are surprised by the suggestion of a period of abstinence since their objective is to cut down on alcohol, as opposed to quitting altogether. However, as you will discover, alcohol free time is an integral part of the moderation journey and research by Jalie Tucker, professor of psychology at Auburn University and author of *Changing Addictive Behaviour,* cites that becoming abstinent for a period is one of the key techniques used by people who successfully moderate their drinking. The distance allows you to see patterns more clearly and by stepping back people are often astonished by the new perspectives they acquire.

In this chapter we discuss the multiple benefits of taking breaks from alcohol, as well as what the experience has been like for other people. You will also be given the skills that you may need to manage during this time. For many people this can be a little daunting because drinking alcohol has become a daily pursuit. However, undergoing a temporary spell of abstinence is much more manageable than contemplating never drinking again and the benefits you will experience are compelling. If you don't feel ready for a month alcohol-free yet, there are other valuable actions you can take, including: a day or two without alcohol; or tapering down, as featured later in this chapter.

SIMON, 33 ACHIEVED A MONTH ALCOHOL-FREE

"I have the abstinence experience to look back on now, to remind me how much happier and healthier I was physically and mentally during that time. It doesn't take me long to remember which side of the coin I want to be on! For me, experiencing an alcohol-free period was a complete game changer on my moderation journey."

The Benefits of Taking a Break from Alcohol

- A month off lowers your tolerance to alcohol so you can experience and enjoy the relaxing effects when consuming it in healthier quantities. Generally, it takes around thirty days for liver enzymes and neurotransmitters to return to a lower level.

- Abstinence allows you a period unclouded by alcohol to acquire sober coping skills, as well as embedding your cutting down commitment firmly in your mind. You can plan how to integrate it into your life and foster a clear sense of commitment to a healthier future.

- Being free of alcohol for a period allows you to experience emotions more naturally. This gives you the wonderful opportunity to learn how to manage them more effectively and to see patterns as well as problems you might be avoiding through the use of alcohol.

- If you have a feeling that your use of alcohol is slipping out of your grasp, you may be feeling disheartened by the situation. A great many people derive a sense of achievement from accomplishing an alcohol-free period, boosting their confidence to make further positive changes.

• In this period, you will probably have the opportunity to witness the peculiar sight of how you and other people truly behave while intoxicated. This is not possible when you are drinking because alcohol alters our perception and judgement. You will most likely want to avoid heavy drinking situations in general while you are doing the thirty-day alcohol-free period. However, a few mental pictures taken during your abstinence period can be a useful asset.

• During your alcohol-free period you can develop the valuable practice of saying 'No' to alcohol. As a moderate drinker, on many days you won't be drinking at all and when you do, you will have to refuse drinks when you reach your limit.

• When taking a month off, many people rediscover how great life can be without alcohol. They realise that drinking alcohol is often unnecessary and in fact, how many social situations are more enjoyable without it. A break allows emotional equilibrium to be restored and to open your eyes again to how life in general can be handled more easily.

What Does a Month Alcohol-Free Feel Like?

Personal experiences of a month alcohol-free can differ widely. Some people find it a breeze and feel considerably better mentally and physically early on. Other people notice that they develop a sweet tooth; feel a little irritable and nervous in the beginning; or are troubled by thoughts of drinking alcohol. Dr Sarah Jarvis of Drinkaware's medical advisory panel notes,

"Psychological symptoms are quite common and not only if you are a very heavy drinker. You can have short-term issues even with relatively low levels of alcohol consumption if you have been used to drinking very regularly; symptoms can include: irritability; poor concentration; feeling shaky; tiredness; having difficulty sleeping; or experiencing bad dreams."

It is important to remember that these minor discomforts will pass. Overall, people report an increased sense of wellbeing, getting in touch with the person they were before heavy drinking entered their life. Many people enjoy feeling more stable because when they are drinking, life can be more chaotic and being alcohol-free can feel more manageable.

TARA, 43, FELT RENEWED CLARITY AND MOTIVATION BY BEING ALCOHOL-FREE

"About a week into my alcohol-free period, I started to feel so much better mentally, it was as though a fog was lifting from my mind. I felt calmer and happier and started to think that I could create a better life for myself. When I was imprisoned by alcohol, I was trying to cope, stumbling from one day to the next. I can now look ahead and take control of my destiny and feel good about myself. I also feel that I understand what it feels like to be healthy again, which creates a strong motivation to protect my wellbeing by finding a balance with alcohol."

Skills to Manage an Alcohol-Free Month and Beyond

Your alcohol-free month provides you with a concentrated period of learning and experience of a range of abstinence tools. These skills have great value throughout your moderation journey in all the instances in which you choose not to drink.

Tune Into Your Why

As you begin your alcohol-free month it can be very motivating to recall the utterly compelling reasons for you to change your drinking habits. Visualise the life you want to create for yourself, with all the benefits you will enjoy, in moving towards your goals. In your mind, you can start to imagine and experience the positive feelings of accomplishment that you will gain from overcoming this obstacle.

Deal with Cravings for Alcohol

Many people experience significant cravings during their month off alcohol, whereas others have smoother sailing. However, this is a crucial area of competence because it is likely that you will experience urges in the future at times when you have decided not to drink. It is important to remember that urges or cravings are completely normal. Rotgers, author of *Responsible Drinking,* states that they may never go away completely. "They are actually learnt somewhat like the way you learnt to ride a bicycle – through lots of practice." Think about all the times you have paired a fun experience with alcohol, including: at your favourite pub with friends; weddings; parties; family barbecues; or while watching sport. Exactly the same as you have never completely forgotten how to ride a bicycle, you never quite forget all the memories created during your drinking career. However, Cyndi Turner, author of *The Clinician's Guide to Alcohol Moderation* helpfully reminds us that, "Just because we have a thought or feeling doesn't mean that we have to indulge it."

The good news is that you get stronger over time and those recollections will fade as you supplement them with new and different memories as you evolve into your new and healthier identity. Several useful and powerful craving management techniques involve avoidance, distraction and confrontation, which are discussed below.

Avoidance

Avoidance skills lower the chance of a craving arising at the outset, so they are particularly valuable.

1. Reduce stress. Negative emotions play a key role in overdrinking for many people. At least to begin with, you should try to avoid situations that may trigger you to drink reactively. In Chapter 4 on triggers, you will have been hunting for these types of scenarios, yet there may be some you can think of right away, such as visiting a challenging relative, or conflict with a partner.

2. Keep clear of any heavy drinking friends. This can be hard, but remember it is only for a month.

3. Steer clear of the places where you ordinarily drink alcohol, such as particular pubs or restaurants. If your normal route home takes you past an off licence, you may find it useful to go a different way.

4. Take good care of yourself. If you are feeling tired, hungry, or thirsty you may notice a craving developing. At these times, listen to your body and tend to your needs.

5. Make alcohol harder to lay your hands on. You may wish to remove alcohol from the house for the present time or keep only small amounts for guests in a different place than you usually store alcohol. Keep yourself occupied. It is a good idea to make plans during your leisure time, such as getting out of the house to enjoy non-drinking activities. This is especially important if you are an at-home drinker.

Confront Your Cravings

Surf the Urge

Alan Marlett, a leading clinical psychologist in the field of addictive behaviours, developed the concept of urge surfing. He likened cravings to waves with deep breathing as the surfboard that carries you through the wave. This is a useful technique because it can be used anywhere, any time.

Urges often come in the form of an inner voice that encourages you to drink alcohol. For example, "It's only a small beer, I will sip on that one slowly" or "I will be back to alcohol in a month's time so why not have a glass of wine now." Observe this talk for what it is and speak back to the urge. Sometimes what you need most is reassurance from within. An example might be, "Having a break from alcohol now will help me to moderate successfully in the future."

ROB, 28, TALKED BACK TO HIS URGES WHICH HELPED HIM WHEN TEMPTATION CALLED

"I was about a week into my alcohol-free month and it was going well. I invited my friend Andrew over for a casual dinner and catch up on the Friday night. Andrew lived about five miles away and normally drove so I stocked up with alcohol-free beers and other soft drinks. Surprisingly, he arrived by taxi and announced that he fancied a few drinks because he had survived an awful week at work and wanted to blow off some steam and out of his rucksack he produced a large case of beer! I hadn't felt any cravings all week but when someone was right in front of me proffering a cold beer it took quite a bit of willpower to refuse. As I was finishing preparing the food, Andrew took a walk outside for a smoke and I had a few choice words with myself."

"Get stuffed cravings."

"Come on, Rob, you can do this."

"I will not back down, this is my plan and I'm sticking to it."

Giving myself a pep talk really helped give me a boost at a vulnerable point. It helped me to feel stronger and more determined. I cracked open a cold alcohol-free beer, had a good dinner and the urge passed pretty quickly. I felt proud that I had risen to the challenge and emerged victorious."

Wait Out the Cravings

An urge may appear powerful because it tells you that it is making you unhappy now, and that you will stay miserable until the point where you give in to it. However, this is absolutely not true, and the wonderful news is that it will not last.

Focus on Your Long-Term Goals

Spend a little time recalling your Why; the utterly compelling reasons why you embarked on your alcohol moderation journey in the first place. Perhaps it was the pursuit of better mental health, or closer relationships with other people. Keeping these reasons at the forefront of your mind is a very good way to stay motivated and focussed. Each time you resist you become stronger.

Not Ready for a Month Alcohol-Free?

If you feel that you are not ready for taking a month off alcohol, trust your judgement because you are the best person to assess your needs throughout your moderation journey. In this case it can be beneficial to break it down into mini alcohol-free periods to build your skills and confidence.

CLARA, 47, GRADUALLY INCREASED HER ALCOHOL-FREE PERIODS OVER TIME

"Before I started my moderation journey it was quite alarming to realise that I was turning into a daily drinker. It crept up on me slowly and I found that I was pouring myself several glasses of wine after work every night and more at the weekends. I was stuck in this pattern for several years and I had reached a point where I was sick and tired of feeling hungover every day. There was no 'rock-bottom' moment, yet my life was feeling out of control and my work was suffering. I knew I had to change. However, a whole month off alcohol felt unmanageable at that stage. Instead, I built up over time, starting with two days alcohol-free, three and then four. My confidence grew and I realised it wasn't as scary as I thought, and I was so proud of the changes I was making. Furthermore, I noticed that when I was drinking, I wasn't consuming as much either. I progressed to a week and then two weeks. I'm delighted to say that I have now completed a whole month off alcohol, and I feel so much better both physically and mentally and I'm sleeping like a baby too!"

Taper Down

Many people find that it is easier to taper down instead of starting with a month off alcohol. An alcohol-free period does have all the benefits that we have discussed and shortens the process but it is not the only route to moderation. The technique of tapering down for a regular or daily drinker involves cutting back gradually and methodically on the number of days when you consume alcohol, and the amount imbibed during a period of drinking. This requires the development of a schedule to ensure that you can chart your progress towards either a month off or more moderate drinking. The rate at which you cut back should be based on what feels realistic and manageable for you.

Alcohol Withdrawal

It is important to note however that for people who have a physical dependence on alcohol, there should be great caution about cutting down, or stopping too abruptly because there is a real and significant risk of life-threatening seizures. If you start to experience significant alcohol withdrawal symptoms when you stop drinking, medical assistance should be sought for cutting back. As previously discussed, generally this programme is not designed for those people who are physically dependent on alcohol because research shows that abstinence after a medically supervised detoxification programme is potentially a better option in this case.

Your Drinking Journal

For those people who do not feel ready to embark on an alcohol-free month or who are tapering down, keeping a drinking journal or diary is a great tool to help you progress to healthier habits and gain a clear picture of your drinking habits. Rotgers, author of *Responsible Drinking,* highlights the fact that the effect of paying increased attention to your drinking through keeping a diary will help to reduce the amount of alcohol consumed. In your diary, note down on each day what you drink; how much you consume; the circumstances (where you were and who you were with); and how you were feeling at the time.

Many people also utilise the diary as a planning aid to prepare ahead for the week, you may mark certain days down as alcohol-free (AF) and others with the units you intend to consume. This way you can lower your alcohol consumption methodically and feel proud of your progress as you chip away at the units and feel better and better. Keeping a diary will help you stay focussed on what you are doing and what you want to achieve, and research has shown that having specific goals works better than general intentions. Psychology professor Dr Gail Matthews of the Dominican University in California conducted a study on goal setting with almost 270 participants. They found that you are 42 per cent more likely to achieve your goals if you write them down. If you have a situation when you overdrink, note that down in your journal too and apply a problem-solving approach, as detailed below, as to why that situation was different from others. Don't be tempted to record only what happens on the good days because all data is important for your moderation journey.

Lapse Management

Some people find that they fall off the wagon during their alcohol-free month. When you implement new behaviours, it is common to have setbacks and it is important to remember that if you aim for thirty days and you make twenty, you will always have those twenty days of success. It is also important that you don't beat yourself up, or take it as evidence that you won't succeed. Remember, a lapse is an opportunity for learning, so dust yourself off and figure out why it happened. The action of a rational problem-solving approach moves your focus away from remorse towards planning for a stronger future.

Lapse Learning Exercise

Answer the following questions with an open, true heart. Use this exercise to ensure you have a productive learning experience so you can move on with your plans in a positive manner.

1. What was the scenario/emotional state that led to my drinking?

_____

_____

_____

2. What have I learnt?

_____

_____

_____

3. How will I approach the situation differently next time?

_____

_____

_____

Have Fun Without Alcohol

Drinking alcohol can be enjoyable, it is also a social lubricant that assists in breaking down barriers and helps people to socialise. There is nothing wrong with looking forward to and appreciating a drink or two, but the key to success is keeping it in its place. Balance is the key to a joyful life and when alcohol becomes the main source of enjoyment, we will most likely progress to drinking more than we are happy with.

Your alcohol-free month is the time in which you will be able to reconnect with the person you were before overdrinking took hold and many people report taking great joy in the simple pleasures of life once more.

MELISSA, 32, RECONNECTED WITH HER TRUE SELF BY BEING ALCOHOL-FREE

"Parties and social gatherings transpired as a trigger for my overdrinking, so I had to rethink how I spent my leisure time. I realised quite early on in my moderation journey that it was important for me to embrace and develop my interests outside of the arena of socialising with alcohol because this had typically led to disaster!

During my alcohol-free month, I decided to arrange more social activities in places where the focus was not solely on alcohol, such as coffee shops or an outdoor activity. Instead of planning a boozy night out, I found that I enjoyed having friends over for dinner. Sometimes on those occasions if other people were drinking, I had a slight craving, but I knew it would pass so I focussed on the other enjoyable elements of the evening. I made sure that I was well stocked with alcohol-free alternatives too.

Over time I discovered that life can be so much more rewarding when you are not overdrinking. I learned that it was easier to connect with people I didn't really know when I was drinking heavily, yet on the flip side I was less connected to people who I was close to. I became a better friend, more reliable partner and my self-esteem increased tenfold. I realised that I liked my non-drinking and moderate self so much more than the destructive party girl. Something inside me had changed for the better and I knew at that point that this was a new start!"

A List of Fun Things to Do

The following is a list of fun activities people say they enjoy when not drinking.

- Cooking
- Planning a holiday or mini break

- Bike-riding
- Going for a walk and being in nature
- Sewing
- Candle making
- Gardening
- Research
- Reading
- Listening to a podcast or audiobook
- Having a barbecue or picnic
- Being with their pets
- Scrapbooking
- Volunteer work
- Charity shopping
- Look at decorating magazines/decorating
- Antique shopping
- Working out
- Journaling
- Going for brunch/coffee with a friend

Taking Breaks Throughout Your Moderation Journey

Having a month alcohol-free isn't only for the start of your wellbeing regime, you can use breaks at regular intervals when you feel the need for a reset. Many people find that alcohol affects them differently depending on how they are feeling, or what else is going on in their lives. It is important to take a flexible approach and listen to what your body is telling you it needs. When you are facing a particularly stressful period in your life, experiencing anxiety or low mood, having a break until you are feeling emotionally stronger may be a wise decision.

Your Way Forward

The great news is that a month alcohol-free allows you to take control and create space in which you can prepare and plan for your moderate future. During this time, you will have the chance to mentally rehearse the application of your limits in negotiating upcoming events successfully.

This period will bring many benefits, including the experience that life can often be better in many types of situations without alcohol. You will have the chance to practice the many abstinence skills that will also be applicable to alcohol-free days when you are moderating, including the crucial understanding that all cravings pass. When you are ready, set your start date for your month alcohol-free, trust in the process and look forward to the wonderful gift of balance and harmony that you are giving to yourself.

Please go to the webpage www.drinklesslivewell.com to access the hypnosis recording that compliments this chapter entitled; *Embracing Alcohol Free Time.*

PART THREE

Make It Work for the Long Term

Chapter 7

STEP SEVEN:
DEAL WITH ANY LAPSES AND RELAPSES

"It's only a stumble, no need to crumble!"

Tansy Forrest

Exactly as with mastering any new skill, time, patience, and resilience are required. There are very few people who can achieve their goals perfectly, straightaway. There will most likely be an element of trial and error in the process of your behaviour change and you should expect this. In this chapter, you will learn how to deal with lapses and relapses on your journey to freedom, in a rational and proactive way. It is always best to be prepared for these ordinary events on the path to any new goal.

There are two types of drinking mishaps you may encounter. A lapse is an isolated incident where you overdrink, whereas a relapse is a series of slip-ups, where you may revert back to your previous drinking habits for a longer period. Far from being a negative phenomenon, you can reframe these everyday situations into positive learning experiences that will strengthen you and build self-knowledge for the future. These occurrences can be emotionally challenging, yet they may be regarded as the refinement of your moderation skill set. There are several factors that can lead to lapses and or relapses. These are classified as either: drinking alcohol in high-risk situations; a lack of necessary life skills; personal coping capacity; or an imbalanced lifestyle.

High-Risk Situations
High-risk circumstances can involve drinking alcohol or overdrinking in a trigger situation that relates to a particular place, time, group of people, and emotional or physical state. During the early stages of moderation mastery, you will be in a

process of fully developing your understanding of your unique triggers and it is common to uncover them along the way. How you respond to the slip, however, is critical for success and you will be wise to handle the situation differently in the future based on your learning.

Once you have completed the lapse exercise, featured later in this chapter, you may adapt your drinking guidelines in your Alcohol Moderation Action Plan to reflect your new insights.

CAROL, 50, LAPSED BUT DID NOT RELAPSE

Carol, a successful entrepreneur, knew she was drinking excessively when she reached the consumption of two bottles of wine on some evenings. She found her sleep was negatively affected and her weight became more difficult to manage. During her moderation journey, she was absolutely delighted to reduce her drinking to only a couple of glasses of wine each evening. She felt a great sense of achievement and happiness. However, after six weeks of working together she had a lapse that took her by surprise. As a result, she felt confused and really annoyed with herself. In her session with me, Carol described a pub lunch she had attended with her cousins. After lunch, she had caught the bus and felt a craving for more alcohol as she returned home. She drank another bottle of wine at home and in her own words; "I felt I had gone back to my previous ways."

I asked her how the lunch had played out and she said that she had ordered a meal that was undercooked, and she had to send it back. Carol didn't want to wait for another meal to be cooked because her family were already eating, so she requested a bowl of chips, which she barely touched. Carol said that the staff at the restaurant had been quite unhelpful, and she had found the experience stressful because she had been looking forward to a nice meal with her family. When she reflected on the situation, Carol came to the realisation that the lack of food, combined with the stress of the interaction with the staff had been a trigger for her overdrinking. Discussing how Carol might handle the situation better in the future, she realised that she needed to prioritise her own needs and make sure she requested a proper meal to eat, especially when she was drinking alcohol. In addition, Carol wanted to be more mindful of stress and the interaction of all these factors. We also discussed the twelve-step acronym of HALT – are you hungry, angry, lonely or tired? These can all be major triggers for many people. To her credit, Carol prevented her lapse from becoming a relapse and with agreed strategies in place, she returned and adhered to her Alcohol Moderation Action Plan. She did not go back to her old ways.

Life Skills

Another reason for a lapse is not having the necessary life skills in a particular area, such as coping with anger or stress. Personal coping skills can be behavioural or cognitive and may include strategies to manage high-risk situations, such as assertiveness training and turning down drinks in social settings. Additionally, these may feature broader strategies that can improve coping with other more varied situations, including: anger management techniques, assertiveness, mindfulness meditation, and positive self-talk. We can all learn new skills to help us manage our lives more easily, so if you feel you need to develop in a particular area make it a priority to reach out for the guidance and support that will help you progress. There are lots of good books that feature these subjects, or you may find it helpful to talk with a therapist.

LUKE, 35, WHOSE LAPSE LED TO LEARNING NEW LIFE SKILLS

Luke, a teacher, had been successfully moderating his drinking for several months when he and his wife had their first child. They were delighted with the new arrival, but they struggled to cope with the sleepless nights along with many additional domestic and caring responsibilities. Furthermore, there were now financial strains on Luke, as the sole breadwinner in the family. In this stressed situation, Luke became irritable and short-tempered with his wife and they had more arguments than before. Luke began to drink more heavily, his alcohol intake slowly crept up until he was drinking a bottle of wine a night. When he came back to see me, he was feeling frustrated and disappointed about his setback. Through our discussion he came to recognise that he had been using alcohol as an emotional crutch to deal with his stress and anger. Luke realised that he needed to use healthier coping strategies to deal with conflict. Luke learnt several simple, but effective anger management techniques he could use in his daily life to help him feel less frustrated and improve his interpersonal relationships with his partner. He took a month off from drinking alcohol to reassess his situation, and fully embed the new techniques. This time alcohol-free gave his mind and body a rest from the excess alcohol.

When Luke was ready to resume his moderation plan, he found it much easier to stick to healthy limits and he was stronger in his resolve because he gained more self-awareness and life skills in the process.

Live a Balanced Life

Another potential cause of a drinking lapse or relapse can be a hidden factor, such as an imbalanced lifestyle, which can lead to urges or cravings. These can be harder to figure out because they may be due to negative life experiences or unresolved stress compounding over time. The essence of the problem is an imbalance of the positive and negative experiences in your life combining until they cause an excessive drinking episode. In the absence of alternative pleasures, people may feel that an indulgence is justified, saying to themselves for example, "I deserve a drink." They may see drinking alcohol as the only route to gain immediate pleasure, gratification, and to escape suffering. One way of dealing with this situation is to increase self-care and to spend more time doing activities you enjoy, find rewarding, or nurturing. The next chapter will allow you to explore this topic in further detail because it is an essential part of mastering moderation and will help you to maintain your positive changes for the long term.

ANDREW, 45, WHOSE LAPSE RESULTED IN RELAPSE

Andrew, a successful businessman, was drinking about 80 units per week. By following his moderation plan with much dedication, he lowered his consumption to an impressive 15 units per week. He lost weight and felt so much healthier. He slept better and felt more connected to his family. He said that he was calmer and more focussed at work. However, about a year and half after we had worked together to achieve this goal, he returned for therapy because he had returned to his previous drinking habits and was feeling tired, frustrated and angry. This was a lapse that had progressed into a relapse, spanning a couple of months. We discussed what had been going on in Andrew's life and he explained that he was feeling very stressed because his workload had greatly increased in recent months. He had not had time to go on holiday with his family and had been working very long hours. Furthermore, his wife had been having a difficult time at work and he was supporting her emotionally. On reflection, Andrew realised that his inadequate work-life balance was overwhelming him, and that drinking alcohol had become a daily way of coping with the stress and tiredness after a long day with clients. Andrew also knew he was becoming frustrated and angry in family situations and did not like the person he had become. We talked about how Andrew might find more balance in his daily life and look after himself better. He decided that he was going to take a proper lunch break and eat a healthy and nutritious meal each day. He was also going to delegate more tasks to other staff and take time off at weekends to rest and recharge with his family. Furthermore, Andrew learnt a few simple, but effective anger management techniques to use in his daily life to help him feel less frustrated and improve his interpersonal relationships.

After putting these strategies in place, Andrew coped better at home and communicated his needs in a much healthier way and empathised with the needs of other family members. Through applying a rational problem-solving approach, Andrew was able to learn from the situation and restore equilibrium. He took an entire month off drinking to give himself time to reset his tolerance levels and to take stock of the situation, which allowed him to also reassess his personal drinking guidelines. After this, he went back to his moderation plan and successfully lowered his units to the previous level. The experience made him stronger because it allowed him to gain a full appreciation of how to make moderation work in the longer term, by living a more balanced life. In this way, he had turned the situation around to his advantage and embraced it as a positive learning experience.

The Interplay of Causal Factors

There may be an interplay between multiple factors that cause lapses and relapses. For example, a high-risk situation, such as a party combined with a lack of life skills, such as stress management tools. It is important to identify all the variables in these situations and to apply a rational problem-solving approach.

Negative feelings faced after a lapse in drinking are a

common experience for people in the process of behaviour change. This is known as the Abstinence Violation Effect (AVE), a term coined by the addiction psychologist Alan Marlatt. This is the self-blame, guilt and perceived loss of self-control that a person faces after breaching their own self-imposed rules. Furthermore, when a person views the lapse as being out of their control, they are more likely to progress from a lapse to a relapse. For example, if they view the lapse as a characteristic of a disease it may increase their sense of helplessness. In other words, the way in which we respond to drifting from our objective affects what happens next. We can become stronger, or we can become discouraged leading to a full-blown relapse.

The concept of AVE also characterises the behaviour of dieters who overindulge when they exceed their daily calorie goal, for example and they regard that day as being ruined. They may in turn have negative thoughts such as, "The diet is already out the window so I may as well eat what I like." They continue to overindulge and give up the control they had previously established. How they respond to the situation also determines their likelihood of getting back on track. If they attribute the lapse to a lack of self-control or a character flaw, they are more likely to have trouble staying on course. However, when they make an external affirmation, such as, "I had a really stressful day yesterday and turned to food as a source of comfort. But I will get back on my path tomorrow to a healthier lifestyle" they are taking back control and can get back on track more easily. Therefore, the way that a person evaluates the lapse is central to maintaining their long-term health improvements. It is valuable to become aware of AVE and its power so we are forewarned, regarding drifting from our objectives and how we can reframe a slip-up as a learning experience.

Take a Break

After a lapse, or particularly in the case of a relapse, it may be very helpful to take a month off alcohol. It can be viewed as a lovely safe haven in which you can recover from the detour, nurture yourself and have space and time away from alcohol to tweak your strategy. You may wish to alter your Alcohol Moderation Action Plan, or have a break and come back to things feeling stronger. For many people such breaks are an integral part of the broader moderation journey and can be employed at any stage to support your health and wellbeing.

A Positive Learning Experience

When we put a new plan of action in place it is very common to have setbacks. The crucial message is to learn from each experience, so we can develop our self-awareness and become more resilient next time. Now, dust yourself off and get out your Sherlock Holmes outfit because you will need to play the detective. The action of problem-solving turns your focus away from regret and towards thinking about the future in a more positive manner.

Complete the following exercise, writing down your answers so you can refer to it later to help you in the future, as you accrue self-knowledge regarding your triggers for overdrinking.

Learn From A Lapse Exercise

Answer the following questions with an open, true heart and with total self-honesty. You do not need to show or share your answers with anyone else. But you want to use this exercise to ensure you have a positive learning experience.

1. What led to the lapse or relapse?

_____

_____

2. What have I learnt from this?

_____

_____

3. What will I do differently in the future?

_____

_____

Focus on Progress Rather Than Perfection

During the process of changing your behaviour you need to go easy on yourself. It is understandable that you want to overcome this issue as soon as you can, but remember that these habits have taken years to develop and it takes time for all of us to permanently establish healthier behaviour patterns. Many people find that lapses occur more frequently at the beginning of the moderation journey. However as more self-knowledge is accrued, over time the lapses become less frequent and self-confidence builds as progress is made and maintained.

STUART, 36, COLLECTED PERSONAL LAPSE DATA

Stuart, a media executive, tended to binge drink in social situations because there was an expectation of wining and dining his clients and attending alcohol-laden work functions. He was always the last person to leave these events and he drank so heavily that it took him several days to fully recover. For as long as he could remember he had been the life and soul of the party, but it left him feeling anxious and exhausted. Around this time, he had a pivotal moment where he found himself dancing in a nightclub, drunk with people from work. He surveyed the scene and had an unexpected moment of clarity, when he realised that he simply did not want to do this anymore. He was determined to make a change!

At the start of his moderation journey lapses were commonplace. Each time it happened, he proactively reflected on the situation to assess variables that had contributed to the lapse to increase his self-knowledge. Over a period of about six months, he managed to lower the binge episodes from four to one per month. The binges themselves also decreased in severity. For Stuart, this was huge progress. It was truly motivating for him to see how his behaviour altered over time. He said that he could feel himself changing and once that happened there was no going back.

Your Way Forward

Lapses, although challenging in nature, are often an integral part of the behavioural change process. When you experience a lapse never allow yourself to feel demotivated, instead focus on the progress you have made so far. Draw a line under a single instance of overdrinking instead of allowing it to snowball into a relapse. Consider taking a break from alcohol to help you reset and build your confidence for your next try. Always apply a rational problem-solving approach to turn the situation into a positive learning experience, which will make you stronger for the future.

Chapter 8

STEP EIGHT:
SELF-CARE AND LIVING A BALANCED LIFE

"Caring for myself is not self-indulgence, it is self-preservation."

Audre Lorde

Mastering moderation is not simply about cutting down on alcohol, it is the creation of a life that is balanced and nourishing. Self-care is the steps you take to tend to your physical and emotional health in the ways that you are best able. It is the underpinning foundation of a healthy existence and of maintaining stable moderation. In this chapter we will explore how you can tend to your mind and body with regularity, helping you to feel a great deal better and become the very best version of yourself. The exact nature of self-care is different for everyone and will change over time according to the ebb and flow of your life.

You might like to think about moderation mastery as having parallels with the creation of a beautiful garden. The intention to change and the techniques and strategies are like the seeds that we plant in the soil. The growth and establishment of healthy strong plants rests on the nurturing they are given along the way. It is the cultivation over the longer term that allows the flowers to flourish and bloom to their fullest potential.

In essence, the more meaningful, happy and fulfilled your life is, the more the desire to fill the gaps will diminish. You will also carry over the positive feelings of wellbeing into your interactions with other people. Caring for yourself means that you can better care for others too. The benefits are broad and have been linked to positive health outcomes such as: reduced stress, an improved immune system, increased productivity and higher self-esteem, according to Brighid Courtney, faculty member at the Wellness Council of America.

SELF CARE DIAGRAM

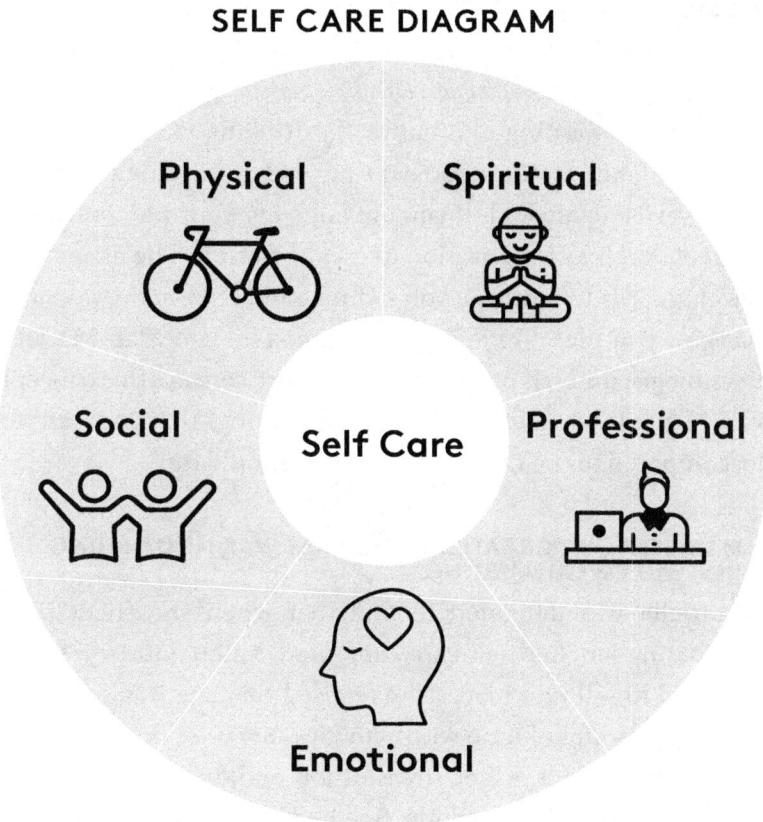

As alcohol is put firmly in its place a whole new world of opportunities is open to you. In this chapter you will have the chance to survey these five domains of your life: physical; social; emotional; spiritual; and professional, to see how you may hone some areas to enhance your wellbeing and maintain good mental and physical health. Pause your reading now; and consider how you are balancing each of these five domains, as shown in the diagram on the previous page.

Rotgers of *Responsible Drinking* also reminds us that developing rewarding alternatives to drinking is an important counterbalance to the effort you put into restraining yourself from overusing alcohol. If you are enjoying your life more, you will feel much less motivation to escape from it. The essence of this chapter is to motivate you to find and increase the pursuits that give you pleasure and satisfaction. The late Alan Marlett, psychologist and relapse prevention expert, conveys this concept well. "The idea is to increase the ratio of things that you want to do, compared to the things you feel you should do."

MARIELLA, 40, CREATED A LIFE THAT WAS NOURISHING INSTEAD OF EXHAUSTING

Mariella was delighted to find that when she spent time focussing on her self-care, her moderation journey really started to fall into place. She realised that she was spending a huge amount of time with activities that were depleting her, namely working in her stressful job and drinking to relieve the pressure of her vocation. She had intense periods of work and late nights working towards many deadlines. This had the effect of narrowing the focus of her life considerably and her exercise routine went out of the window. After a big job was complete, she blew off steam with a drinking session, but this led to her feeling anxious and tired in the days afterwards. Over time she made small changes by moving the focus, via her self-care, towards activities that nourished her and fitted them into her schedule, even when work was busy. She started to make exercise a priority and made sure she took a gym class three times a week. In addition, she started to think about the activities that had made her happy in her childhood, such as: walking in nature; flower arranging; and spending time by the sea. Cooking was also something she had enjoyed greatly and baking had been very special to her as a young girl. She made a conscious effort to reclaim these lost arts and she began by spending time outdoors in nature, sometimes going for a jog or for a gentle walk. Furthermore, with the money she saved on alcohol over a few months she booked a long overdue mini-break to the seaside, staying at a gorgeous little hotel overlooking the water. These changes had the wonderful effect of shrinking the significance of the role that alcohol played in her life as she was rediscovering more varied ways to enjoy herself, to be creative and allow her personality to shine. For Mariella, it was about creating an existence that was nourishing and gave her the mental space to be happy and healthy without pushing herself to her emotional and physical limits, which in the past led her to self-medicate with alcohol. When she experienced a life that was happier and more balanced, she found that drinking lapses were reduced drastically. Consequently she enjoyed herself so much more and had increased energy to be productive in all areas of her life.

Balance Elements of Nurture and Depletion in Your Daily Life

In this first activity you will have the chance to evaluate aspects of your life that deplete you and those that nourish you. It is a great idea to regularly reflect on the balance between the two because this will ensure that you can deal with life's difficulties more easily and have better mental health overall.

A few activities we do in the day might be considered as nurturing activities. These pursuits can restore us and renew our emotional and or physical reserves of energy. They can improve our mood and allow us to manage stressful situations more easily and reduce our need for alcohol in many cases. Other activities may be depleting and drain our emotional and/or physical energy, increase stress and take away from our feelings of happiness. When life becomes too busy or we experience a stressful life event, it can be common to give nurturing activities a back seat. We can forget that they help us to feel better and to maintain our physical and emotional wellbeing.

Nurturing Activities

- Having healthy, regular meals and snacks if required.
- Spending time outside in nature.
- Ensuring enough good quality sleep.
- Taking days off work and having holidays.
- Engaging in your hobbies.
- Meditating and/or listening to hypnosis recordings.
- Taking lunch breaks/regular work and computer breaks.
- Socialising with friends.
- Exercise.

Depleting Activities

- Caring for other people.
- Interacting with emotionally needy or draining family members/friends or colleagues/customers or patients.
- Reading the news, social media, online platforms.
- Ruminating or dwelling on the past.
- Doing chores.
- Travelling/commuting.

MAINTAIN BALANCE EXERCISE

1. Note down your current daily activities in the first column from the moment you wake to the time you go to sleep.

2. Evaluate if these activities are either depleting or nurturing and place a tick in either column, accordingly.

3. Look at the balance between nurture and depletion in your day. Are you able to take any actions to create more equilibrium, if necessary, by adding in more nurturing activities? Or perhaps you might like to structure your day differently to further support your wellbeing?

4) Use the New Daily Structure below to plan the changes.

Current Daily Activities

Activity	Depleting	Nurturing

New Daily Activities

Activity	Depleting	Nuturing

Other general actions I can take to restore balance in my life. You may wish to consider planning days off and/or holidays in this list too.

1.

2.

3.

4.

5.

Well done! I recommend checking and retaking this inventory once a month. Having your finger on the pulse in relation to where you are expending your physical and emotional energy is the key to living a full and balanced life.

Good Quality Sleep

Sleep is the foundation on which all aspects of health and wellbeing rest. According to Graham Lawton, author of *This Book Could Save Your Life,* there is no physical or mental process that is not improved by sleep or impaired by lack of it. Sleep is as vital for life as food and water. Many of my clients report they sleep for longer and more deeply over time as they cut down on alcohol.

Alcohol disturbs sleep in complicated ways. Some people find that alcohol seems to help them sleep. Alcohol is a sedative, but sedation is not sleep and unfortunately the effects of alcohol do not stop there. It is all too easy to mistake one for the other. The use of alcohol to encourage sleep is not advised because it will create further problems down the line. William Miller, author of the useful handbook, *Controlling Your Drinking: Tools to Make Moderation Work for You,* points out that if you are sleeping with alcohol in your bloodstream, you may not get enough of the deepest, most rejuvenating type of sleep. In addition, consuming alcohol seems to make it more likely that a person will be restless during sleep and will wake more frequently during the night. As a result, you may wake in the morning feeling unrested.

Alcohol affects everyone differently and sleeping patterns and requirements are also often unique to the individual and depend on age. However, we can confidently assume that as you lower your alcohol intake and have fewer drinking days your sleep will improve overall, your mood will be more consistent, and you will have more energy to be productive and enjoy your day. Your appetite and food choices will also improve. Many people report that good self-care is cumulative. For example, taking regular exercise helps you to sleep better, which cascades into improvements in your eating patterns. Each positive step affects another area of your life favourably.

MICK, 38, MADE GOOD SLEEP A PRIORITY AND WAS REWARDED WITH UNEXPECTED BENEFITS

Mick found that focussing on a great night's rest was a key aspect of his self-care routine. Naturally over time as his alcohol intake lowered, he enjoyed much better quality sleep. He spent time researching to find sleep meditations that he enjoyed. He found recordings that helped him to become grounded in the present moment and to focus on his breathing were extremely nourishing. This allowed him to release stress and let go of any emotional burden accrued during the day. He also enjoyed listening to my sleep hypnosis recordings and discovered that he could drift off to sleep more quickly when he put one on before bed. Another bonus of listening to the hypnosis before sleep was that he felt they improved his mood the next morning. He reported waking up feeling refreshed and positive, ready for a great day. Further to this, Mick discovered that his bouts of low energy after his binge drinking and disturbed sleep were rapidly becoming an aspect of his past. As a result, he was able to enjoy regular runs again, which increased his fitness. This exercise was a great source of enjoyment and gave him a natural high, which he found to be ten times more rewarding than any alcohol-based activities.

How to Ensure a Good Night's Sleep

The following are my suggestions for good sleep hygiene, which simply means creating an environment that promotes sleep and minimises the chances of being woken.

Go to bed at the same time

Try to go to sleep and wake up at the same time, even if you aren't really tired or don't have to get up early. The time you wake in the morning is the most important aspect of this because it allows the sleep pressure to accrue during the day.

Keep your bedroom cool

According to Lawton, your body's core temperature needs to decrease by 1.2 degrees to get to sleep. You may have noticed that it takes longer to fall asleep when you are in a hot room. The optimum is 18.5 degrees and it may feel colder than you might expect. Wearing socks to bed might be helpful in this case.

Let darkness fall

As the last hour before bed approaches, you can aid the natural production of the sleep hormone, melatonin, by dimming or turning off as many lights as possible and keeping screen time on devices to an absolute minimum or preferably not at all. Use table lamps with warm toned light bulbs rather than bright overhead lights.

Enjoy a relaxing sleep ritual

Create a relaxing bedtime routine that might involve a selection of the following ideas.

- Give yourself a gentle hand and/or foot massage.

- Do gentle body stretching that feels good for you.
- Read a pleasant book that is not overly stimulating.
- Listen to a meditation or sleep hypnosis as you drift off to sleep. (You can find a huge selection on my YouTube channel).

Create a dark and quiet space

Invest in comfy earplugs because even if low level noise doesn't wake you, it can still pull you out of deep sleep into a lighter phase. A sleep mask or blackout curtains are also an excellent investment to help you get the good quality sleep you need to feel your best.

Night-time waking

An issue that many people face is waking up in the night and feeling as though you can't get back to sleep. It may be useful for you to know that waking is perfectly normal and evidence suggests that this increases as we age. You may wake briefly as the body goes through several sleep cycles of deep and light slumber during the night. It is important to note that because you have woken it doesn't mean you will stay awake. You may have experienced a time when you have thought to yourself, "Oh I've woken up now and it's going to be impossible to go back to sleep again." This causes unnecessary anxiety, so how about reframing that situation as, "Oh I'm awake, that's normal and natural sometimes, and I will be asleep again soon." You may find it helpful to focus on your breathing, no need to change your breathing. Simply focus on your breath going in and out of your body, visualise letting go of your thoughts like leaves floating down a stream and you will drift off again as your body relaxes.

You may also like to listen to a body scan meditation or other sleep hypnosis track to help you drop off gently, particularly if you find yourself prone to overthinking at night.

If after a longer period of wakefulness, say half an hour, you can't get back to sleep, you may need to get up and have a reset. You may find having a hot milky drink is helpful as it gently lowers your core body temperature, calming your nervous system and creating a sense of comfort and nurturing. Try doing something relaxing like a jigsaw, reading or listening to an audio book until such time as you feel tired and can relax into sleep once again.

Learn to Relax and Let Go of Stress

Research tells us that the reason people often drink alcohol is to relax, feel good or change their mood. In moderate doses alcohol does allow us to relax to some extent. However, in larger doses and when used too frequently it can produce negative side effects. Due to the way that the nervous system in our bodies is structured, psychological and physical tension are interconnected and the more tense you feel the more your muscles tighten up. Conversely, the more your muscles tighten, the more tense you feel. Therefore, it is very beneficial to use other ways to relax and feel at ease. This helps you to balance levels of tension and relaxation in your life.

The following are my suggestions that you may wish to incorporate into your life. The next time you think that you need a drink to deal with stress, or relax, why not ask yourself what else you can do instead?

Have a massage

Massage is potentially one of the oldest of the healing and relaxing traditions. An immediate beneficial effect of massage is a feeling of very deep relaxation and serenity. The practice of massage stimulates the release of endorphins that produce feelings of calm, as well as reducing stress hormones, such as adrenaline and cortisol, which has a beneficial effect on our immune system.

Mindfulness

Mindfulness is the practice of being in full awareness of whatever is occurring in the present moment, without judging or filtering. It is the cultivation of an awareness of the body and mind as experienced in the here and now. Practising mindfulness regularly leads to positive brain changes. A *Psychiatry Research* study revealed that eight weeks of mindfulness training led to changes in grey matter concentrations in the brain areas involved with: learning and memory processes; emotion regulation; self-referential processing; and perspective taking. You reap the benefits of mindfulness whether you are actively doing it or not.

The roots of mindfulness can be traced back to ancient Buddhist traditions of meditative practice, yet elements of being mindful and present are central ideas in many religions including Judaism and Christianity. Mindfulness can be practiced in two distinct ways, either formally or informally. A formal practice relates to the action of taking time out of your day for a given period to sit or lie and place your focus on your: breathing; the sensations within your body; your physical senses; your thoughts; or your emotions. Informal practise allows us to bring mindful awareness to any daily activity or circumstance, you may already be familiar with mindful eating, walking or drinking.

The benefits of mindfulness are that it allows us to reside more fully in the here and now instead of our mind's tendency to be rehearsing and rehashing life's events. And it is this disidentification with the business of the thinking mind that can help us to find greater peace and acceptance in our lives. Elisha Goldstein, author of *A Mindfulness-Based Stress Reduction Workbook* states that, "It can be quite challenging to remain an impartial observer when you sit in a hall of mirrors, face-to-face with your fear, shame, guilt and other unwelcome yet familiar internal visitors." However, he argues that the practice allows us a space to step outside of this parade of mental wounds, aversions and fantasies and simply observe them as they come and go. Over time with regular mindfulness practises, you can be the observer of the thinking mind and experience much more profound states of acceptance and peace. As we come to understand life as a flowing river of constant change, you may start to appreciate all aspects of the lived experience, including: pain; joy; and fear, with less stress and more equilibrium. We can miss out on so much when we are caught up with the anticipation of the future or rumination about past events. Living a more mindful life is an antidote to this mode of thinking and will allow you to: harness better sleep; increase self-esteem; reinvigorate your enthusiasm for life and your work; and help you to feel calmer and happier generally.

There are many mindfulness meditation recordings that you can find on the Internet which can be used alongside your hypnosis recordings for maximum benefit. They are often short, yet are a supportive and powerful practice that will permit you to perceive how you are feeling emotionally, physically and mentally. This understanding will help you recentre yourself in the present time and place, as well as to disidentify from the river of incessant thoughts.

Spend time in nature

Known by many people these days as nature bathing or the green prescription, physicians in the Shetland Islands have been recommending wilder options for patients alongside their conventional treatment programmes. Graham Lawton states that those people with a range of mental and physical ailments are being encouraged to take up outdoor activities, such as: hiking; beach combing; and in some cases, cloud spotting. The objective of this is not to increase exercise levels but instead is about immersing themselves in nature. Further research on this topic is compelling and Lawton indicates that a similar initiative in New Zealand revealed that six to eight months after receiving the green prescription, two thirds of patients had increased their physical activity levels, felt healthier and had lost weight. Furthermore, a range of immunity and cardiovascular benefits have been purported by the practice of *Shinrin-Yoku,* popular in China and Japan. Also known as Forest Bathing, this refers to walking gently through the forest, breathing deeply and taking in and enjoying the sights and sounds of nature through all the physical senses, including: sight; sound; smell; taste; and touch.

If you cannot get out into nature very frequently, listening to my hypnotherapy narratives that feature scenes and sounds from the natural world may also be beneficial in lowering blood pressure and heart rate. But, if possible, do both because spending time in nature is highly beneficial for everyone; especially for mental health by reducing the stress response as the heart rate slows down and we breathe better. Ideally, a two-hour period should be spent in nature per week for maximum physical and psychological benefit, which can be broken down into smaller chunks. You may decide to combine some or part of it with exercise to maximise the benefits of the experience.

Exercise

Building up and sustaining regular exercise has many overall benefits for the mind and body and will help you enhance your moderation journey. It will keep you slim and young as well as garnering protection from heart attacks, strokes, diabetes, Alzheimer's, and depression. Many types of exercise may also stimulate the same endorphin rewards systems as alcohol does. Many of my clients report that exercise helps them to deal with stress by reducing its intensity much more effectively than alcohol.

An important finding came from a study by Morris and Crawford on the iconic double decker buses in London, in 1953, when buses had conductors as well as drivers. The conductors were running up and down the stairs all day and generally on their feet. A team of medics found that they had half as many heart attacks as their seated driver colleagues.

Rotgers of *Responsible Drinking* points out that exercise gives us a tangible feeling of health and wellbeing, relieves stress and can benefit sleep. This feeling of physical improvements can reinforce heightened feelings of mental control and general feelings of competence. The key is to do something you like and establish the routine of doing it regularly. It doesn't have to be every day; three times a week is manageable for most people. To increase your motivation for healthy living and exercise, why not listen to my hypnosis for weight loss and exercise motivation on YouTube. Pop this on while you sit in bed with your morning drink and it will supercharge your day with positive affirmations and a narrative to really get you going. A recent analysis of data from 36,370 people aged forty plus, featured in the *British Journal of Sports Medicine* and conducted by Perreault et al found that people who drank alcohol moderately and completed at least 7.5 hours of activity per week, decreased their risk of death from heart disease and cancer significantly.

ASSESS YOUR SELF-CARE ACTIVITY

Implementing balanced self-care is an incredibly effective way of enhancing your wellbeing, supporting good mental health, and making your moderation journey work for the long term. Many aspects of self-care can be part of your daily and weekly routine, such as spending time preparing healthy balanced meals, visiting the gym, taking walks in nature or other forms of exercise. The following activity gives you the opportunity to assess the consistency and quality in your five key life spheres.

1) Physical   4) Professional and/or sense of purpose

2) Social   5) Spiritual

3) Emotional

In the boxes provided, rate your frequency or competency in each activity, using the key featured below. Please note that some activities may not be appealing to you or appropriate to your individual life situation. I have also left space so you can add your own ideas at the bottom.

0 I never do this   *I'm not good at doing this*
1 I sometimes do this   *I'm okay at doing this*
2 I do this very often   *I'm good at this*
* I'm keen to do this more frequently *This is an area for development*

Physical Self-Care

_____ I rest when I'm unwell.

_____ I drink plenty of water throughout the day.

_____ I have good quality sleep.

_____ I take regular exercise.

_____ I eat regular balanced meals and healthy snacks if and when required.

_____ I eat a moderate amount of treats, such as: chocolate; or fast foods.

_____ I go to my dental and GP appointments and take medication as needed.

_____ I go to other physical therapists such as: osteopath; physiotherapist; or chiropractor as needed.

_____ I spend time in nature.

_____ I understand the components of a healthy balanced diet.

Social Self-Care

_____ I have healthy boundaries in my friendships and/or with my family members.

_____ I engage in mentally stimulating discussions with others.

_____ I spend quiet, private time with my partner, such as: going on a regular date night; or date day.

_____ I have space and time to be intimate and romantic with my partner.

_____ I spend time with friends and/or family.

_____ I ask for assistance when I need it.

_____ I create new friendships and talk to new people.

_____ I engage in fun group or community activities.

Emotional Self-Care

_____ I can express my feelings and or emotions by talking or journaling.

_____ I seek help from a therapist when I feel that I need additional emotional support for anxiety, depression, or other emotional worries, which are affecting the quality of my life.

_____ I enjoy hobbies.

_____ I frequently practice nurturing activities, such as: a long bath; having a massage; a gentle walk in nature; going for a spa day.

_____ I take days off from my work and or responsibilities.

_____ I unplug from social media and or emails.

_____ I have separate work and personal telephones.

_____ I go on holiday or mini breaks.

_____ I can kick back and have a laugh.

Professional and/or Sense of Purpose Self-Care

_____ I have and maintain a pleasant and comfortable working environment.

_____ I seek support or assistance when required.

_____ I feel valued and encouraged by those people who manage or supervise my work.

_____ I bond and/or socialise with workmates.

_____ I balance my work and leisure time.

_____ I turn down unreasonable tasks.

_____ I accept interesting and/or stimulating projects when asked.

_____ I take lunch breaks and regular work breaks.

_____ I pursue further professional development opportunities.

_____ I seek reward, promotion and or recognition when it is deserved.

_____ I initiate interesting projects and am supported in these endeavours.

_____ I have adequate time to complete my work tasks.

Spiritual Self-Care

_____ I have peaceful time for personal reflection.

_____ I practice gratitude.

_____ I regularly meditate.

_____ I listen to hypnosis.

_____ I explore spiritual topics by reading or attending group events.

_____ I engage in religious and or spiritual practices of my choosing.

_____ I have time and space to appreciate beauty in literature, art, or the
natural world.

_____ I volunteer for my community or a charity.

Areas for Development

1.

2.

3.

Your Way Forward

Identifying and moving forward with positive life alterations is likely to be new territory, yet over time you will be amazed how much you want to explore, once you allow yourself to create equilibrium in your life. At first it may feel as though nothing will be as fun as alcohol, when really it is that nothing is as comfortable or routine as alcohol. Stick with it and you will create new routines that you love more. Remember, the next chapter to your life has not been written yet. We all have the right to make positive changes and create a healthier future, regardless of our past.

The key is to make incremental progress towards a healthier life over time, rather than trying to overhaul all aspects at once. In the future you can keep coming back to these activities and honing different areas. After all, good self-care is a lifelong process that needs reflection and maintenance for all of us.

As we tap into alcohol-free pursuits, we discover or rediscover the true essence of life. As the physical, intellectual, social, and emotional aspects of your life are realised, the attraction of alcohol becomes less of a focus. Liberation from the grip of overdrinking enables you to come back to living your best life, where your finest capabilities are realised.

Chapter 9

STEP NINE:
NEED A HELPING HAND? NALTREXONE AND THE SINCLAIR METHOD

"Medication-assisted treatment for alcohol use disorder offers a path to recovery that doesn't require abstinence as the starting point."

Dr. David Sinclair

During your alcohol moderation journey, as with life in general, it is beneficial to reflect on your progress towards your goals and your sense of happiness and satisfaction overall. By this point you will no doubt be making improvements to your alcohol consumption level and reaping the benefits. Many of my one-to-one clients find that the programme you have implemented from the guidance of this book, combined with the hypnotherapy recordings, are conducive to bring about permanent positive changes to health and wellbeing.

However, this chapter is for you if you feel within your heart that you need an extra helping hand – in the form of medication – to further assist you in meeting your happy place with alcohol. An increasing proportion of my clients have integrated medication into their moderation journey with excellent results, namely, The Sinclair Method. They have experienced a decrease in consumption and overall interest in alcohol, as well as increased feelings of control over alcohol. A miracle treatment you may think! Well, it is modern science that makes this possible.

The Sinclair Method

TSM as it is otherwise known was developed by the late Dr. David Sinclair PhD who began studying behavioural reinforcement in the 1960s. His pioneering method involves taking a drug called naltrexone or nalmefene one hour before drinking alcohol. This medication can support people who are looking to reduce drinking alcohol. It works by blocking the brain's opioid receptors – where endorphins normally bind to create that familiar sense of reward when we drink.

According to Sinclair, alcohol use disorder is a conditioned response. People become conditioned to drink alcohol because of its actions in the brain in much the same way that Pavlov's dogs became conditioned to salivate at the sound of a bell.

Alcohol is widely available and socially acceptable, so we have frequent opportunities to drink, triggering an endorphin release in our brain. Endorphins are the happy chemicals that allow us to learn new conditioned responses. Ordinarily, this is a positive action as conditioned reactions aid us in survival. However, Kenneth Anderson, author of the influential book, *How to Change Your Drinking* reminds us that in the case of alcohol, the conditioned response may lead us to perpetuate a bad habit. The endorphins that are released when we consume alcohol reinforce the drinking behaviour and this can lead to alcohol use disorder in some people. Furthermore, Cyndi Turner, author of *The Clinician's Guide to Alcohol Moderation* states that the more that the synapses in the brain grow, the more a person thinks about and craves alcohol.

David Sinclair deduced that the opiate antagonist (blocking) medication would, over time, weaken and extinguish the craving by blocking the reinforcing effects of alcohol on the brain. This is known as pharmacological extinction. His findings were tested and published in the 1980s. The book, *The Cure for Alcoholism* by Roy Eskapa PhD, who worked with Dr. Sinclair is a useful guide for those people who decide to embark on TSM to complement their moderation journey.

Furthermore, the late Dr Stewart Leavitt, an important voice in the addiction field, reviewed 14 clinical trials conducted between 1992–2001 of more than 2000 participants in five countries regarding the efficacy of naltrexone in the treatment of alcohol dependence. He concluded that there is strong evidence that naltrexone significantly reduces relapses to heavy drinking, the frequency and quantity of alcohol consumption, as well as alcohol craving.

The American actress Claudia Christian who suffered from alcohol use disorder achieved great personal success with TSM and was compelled to dedicate herself to the cause. Christian served as the executive producer and narrator of the highly-informative documentary *One Little Pill* and has also set up the C Three Foundation to bring awareness to TSM. Her Ted Talk about the subject to date has had more than 4.7 million views.

Why You Haven't Heard of TSM Before

There is ongoing global debate about how the drug should be taken to treat addiction issues. In accordance with TSM, one naltrexone or nalmefene tablet is taken one hour before you intend to drink alcohol and you do not take the medication when you have an alcohol-free day. According to Dr David Sinclair (2001) there is "abundant evidence suggesting that the combination of naltrexone (or nalmefene) and drinking — thus allowing pharmacological extinction — is an effective tool in alcoholism treatment that eventually allows patients to regain better control over their alcohol consumption."

This is in sharp contrast with the UK National Institute for Health and Care Excellence (NICE) current recommendation that naltrexone may be administered daily to patients. It is also currently listed on the NHS website for alcohol use disorder treatment without specifying how often and when it should be taken. The Sinclair Method is not currently as well recognised in the UK as it is in the USA where it is a mainstream medication.

The disadvantage of taking naltrexone or nalmefene every day as per the current NICE guidelines is that the drug will extinguish every behaviour that creates the production of endorphins. This will reduce your enjoyment of: exercise; listening to music; being in nature; eating spicy foods; sex; and basically anything that brings personal joy. You might argue that these are exactly the behaviours we want to be engaging in to create a more rewarding life on alcohol-free days. However, a further benefit of the TSM approach is that on the days when you are not taking naltrexone and are alcohol-free, you will experience a much more powerful surge of endorphins from healthy behaviours. This will reinforce your healing journey by incentivising you to engage in positive actions that create a richer life on an increasing basis.

As you may remember from Chapter 2, the predominantly Twelve Step rehab industry is highly lucrative for investors in the US, UK and around the world. Continuing with the status quo is therefore in their financial interests because the consumer is contending with a condition that may require multiple bouts of expensive inpatient treatment. In contrast, with TSM, naltrexone or nalmefene is available in a cheap, generic form, which makes this not only a highly-effective treatment for alcohol issues, but also one of the least expensive.

Where Can I Obtain Naltrexone if I Want to Follow The Sinclair Method?

The good news is that TSM is gaining in popularity for obvious reasons. However, not all doctors are familiar with this approach. If you want to follow The Sinclair Method with naltrexone or nalmefene you will have to get a prescription from a private GP who specialises in The Sinclair Method. Please contact me for more information as I work with a doctor in the UK who can advise you further and assess your suitability for this treatment and prescribe naltrexone or nalmefene for use with The Sinclair Method.

If you decide to add medication to your moderation journey it is imperative to do so under the care of a behaviour change specialist such as myself alongside a physician in case of any side effects which may include: vomiting; nausea; headache; or fatigue. Most side effects are transitory and mild, usually occurring only at the outset of treatment as the body gets used to the medication.

Naltrexone is processed through the liver and individuals with liver function issues may be adversely affected by taking the medication. In that case nalmefene may be offered as an alternative. Your doctor will use the results of a liver function test as well as your general medical history to help determine which medication is the safest and most appropriate for your individual needs.

Important Notes Regarding Opioid Blocking Medications

If you are recommended naltrexone or nalmefene by a doctor, you should be informed that they will stop pain medication (such as morphine or codeine) or other medications that contain opioids from being effective. If you need painkillers whilst taking the medication (particularly after surgery or dental work) it's very important that you let your doctor or dentist know so they can select a painkiller that will work for you.

It is also recommended that you keep a note in your health app or wallet or use a medical alert bracelet or tag in case of an emergency so that your care team in that instance knows you are taking an opioid blocking medication.

Furthermore, other over-the-counter medications can cause issues, as many remedies for coughs, colds or diarrhoea contain opioids. For example, codeine in cough syrup or loperamide in antidiarrheals like Imodium. Using opioids whilst on naltrexone or nalmefene can make them ineffective or bring on withdrawal symptoms so it is safest to opt for non-opioid medications. Always consult a pharmacist if you are not sure and make your GP aware that you are taking an opioid blocking medication.

TANISHA, 42, REDUCED EXCESSIVE DRINKING, WHILE ACKNOWLEDGING LIMITATIONS OF THE MEDICATION
By incorporating TSM together with hypnotherapy and coaching, Tanisha experienced a greater sense of control when consuming alcohol. She became more mindful of her intake and observed over time, her craving for alcohol decreased

significantly. In the past, alcohol was something she had thought about a lot in daily life, often looking forward to the next drinking session. Yet, she soon found that the naltrexone was doing its job perfectly, because it began to effectively curb her desire to drink.

However, Tanisha also grappled with multiple mental health issues, including OCD and trauma, which led to her experiences of emotional overwhelm and low mood. During times of high anxiety, alcohol became particularly appealing. Through her journey with TSM, Tanisha learned that naltrexone couldn't address emotional dysregulation or intense stress. She worked closely with her therapist to recognise the importance of developing her own alternative coping mechanisms for high-stress situations to avoid alcohol as a means to alter her mindset. She employed strategies including: deep-breathing techniques; managing emotional overwhelm before social engagements; regular exercise for stress relief; as well as consistent therapy sessions.

As a result, Tanisha now feels more able to navigate acute stress periods and make informed decisions about whether to drink or not in such circumstances. She found it was best when she was feeling acutely stressed simply not to drink at all.

While naltrexone helps her to drink more mindfully during calm moments, she acknowledges its limitations in dealing with stress, which after all, isn't the medication's function. Tanisha continues to use naltrexone when she drinks alcohol, understanding that it is only one component of her holistic approach to feeling her happiest and healthiest self.

Achieve the Best Results

To begin the method, and your doctor will guide you with this, it is often recommended to gradually build up your body's acceptance to the full 50mg dose and minimise any side effects. For example, taking half a 50mg tablet for a few days when you drink alcohol, until you feel comfortable taking the full dose. As with all medication, the body takes a little time to get used to it. Most side effects are transitory, but your doctor can oversee your care on these matters. It is imperative that you take your medication one hour before you intend to drink, make sure you are hydrated, and eat while drinking. And finally, to give you the best outcomes, work with a therapist who is a specialist in TSM to help you make the positive behaviour changes you desire.

Naltrexone needs to be taken for the rest of your life, on the occasions when you choose to drink alcohol, to ensure the problematic pathways in your brain do not reform. Alcohol use disorder can eventually go into remission. However, if you drink alcohol without taking naltrexone in the future, the old issues will return. It is a life-saving medication, but you must have it with you always, in case you decide to drink alcohol. Another tip for success with TSM is to avoid drinking spirits, which are higher in alcoholic volume and harder to manage as part of a healthy lifestyle.

SCOTT, 38, FOUND ABSTINENCE UNSUSTAINABLE BUT TSM GAVE HIM HIS LIFE BACK

Scott lived in London and enjoyed a successful career in the media that involved much wining and dining with clients. Over time he realized it was affecting his health and wellbeing, leading to lengthy periods of recovery where his energy levels were low.

Scott decided to make a career change because he felt that the party lifestyle in London was unsustainable. However, the pressure of this career change, combined with the stress of moving to another country resulted in his return to increased drinking. This led him to spend time in a rehab centre for alcohol. The stay in the inpatient facility acted as a perfect 'circuit breaker' to halt his spiralling drinking at that point in his life, yet at the same time he found Alcoholics Anonymous Twelve Steps of Abstinence restrictive and disempowering.

Scott was looking for an alternative approach because he felt, for him, abstinence was an unsustainable way to live his life long-term. Scott embarked on TSM and worked hard to meet the tablet halfway. He continued to undertake therapy sessions to examine habits and behaviour patterns to create and embed healthy coping strategies to more effectively manage the trials and tribulations of his life. Over time and with strict compliance to the method, Scott found that his desire to drink diminished and he now feels more in control of his alcohol use when socialising. He is at a point where he feels he can take or leave alcohol. He is forever grateful to the method for putting him on a path where he feels he can finally move forward in his life.

Meet the Medication Halfway

The Sinclair Method may be considered a revolutionary approach to treating alcohol use disorder. However, it is important to note that the success of the program hinges not only on the medication but also on active participation and behaviour change commitment to meet the medication halfway. With TSM, achieving lasting results requires a holistic approach through the examination of habits, behaviours and both practical and emotional triggers that have led to destructive drinking patterns in the past. Furthermore, self-care plays a pivotal role in supporting the effectiveness of the program. Reducing stress; boosting energy levels; and finding alternative ways to experience natural endorphins are vital components of recovery.

Additionally, it is important to consider making smart choices about what and when you drink, such as: opting for less concentrated beverages; or diluting them to reduce alcohol intake. Eating a substantial meal before consuming alcohol can also help moderate its effects and ensure that the medication continues to work effectively in reducing alcohol cravings while further minimising the potential to overdrink or binge.

ARTHUR, 62, INCORPORATED TSM WITH GREAT SUCCESS

Arthur had a long-standing struggle with alcohol consumption. He was a daily drinker, often indulging earlier in the evening and again later at night and occasionally binge drinking. His unit consumption was around 80 units per week. His drinking sometimes caused conflict with his wife and children, further exacerbating his drinking habits. Arthur was susceptible to anxiety and stress in both his work and personal life.

In search of help, Arthur reached out for one-on-one sessions. Initially, we employed hypnotherapy and alcohol moderation techniques, which yielded some positive results. However, Arthur found himself slipping back into his old habits as he felt the compulsion to drink was strong. We discussed the introduction of TSM and he took the time to conduct his own research on the topic. Arthur returned with newfound optimism and with the help of a doctor who assessed him and oversaw his medication, he began taking naltrexone following The Sinclair Method. He reached the full 50mg dose over the course of a couple of weeks and always took his medication one hour before drinking alcohol.

The effects of naltrexone were immediately evident because his alcohol consumption decreased over time to 35 units. We continued to combine hypnotherapy with TSM and he successfully lowered his alcohol intake to 20 units. Arthur is now elated with his progress and enthusiastically shares his experience with others.

ARE YOU WHERE YOU WANT TO BE? EXERCISE

Ask yourself the following questions and write your answers down in as much detail as you can. If it helps, discuss your answers with someone you trust, whether someone in your family, a therapist, coach or mentor.

1. Have you read and applied the previous chapters of this book?

2. Do you feel happy with your alcohol moderation progress?

3. Do you need an additional helping hand on your journey?

4. Are you ready to commit and comply with a medication-assisted approach?

5. Have you completed your research on The Sinclair Method?

Your Way Forward

Now, you have had a chance to consider The Sinclair Method, and how it can be beneficial for your moderation journey. I encourage you to do your own research and take the time you need to consider this additional helping hand. When properly applied by meeting the medication halfway and committing to behaviour change, as well as consistently taking the tablet in accordance with the Sinclair approach, it can be a life-saver for so many people. According to Sinclair (2001) there is most likely stronger scientific evidence supporting the use of naltrexone than for using any other medication in the treatment of alcohol use disorder. Following the protocol diligently and staying compliant with the treatment plan is crucial for success. It is therefore essential to understand that The Sinclair Method is not a passive treatment, it requires dedication and active participation. However, with this information you will be empowered to consider your options, make the right choices and become your healthiest and happiest self.

Chapter 10

STEP TEN:
CREATE YOUR FUTURE FOCUS MAP

"We get what we focus on consistently."
Kevin W. Pearson

By this point you will have many techniques in your toolkit to help you cut back your alcohol intake successfully. And now this is where the magic really happens because you can design the life you have always dreamt of! It's time to discover that there is a whole world of possibilities waiting for you as you remove overdrinking from your life. This chapter shows you how to design a Future Focus Map, which allows you to plan the life you really want and the benefits you will enjoy in moving towards your goals.

Why Your *Why* Matters

Your Future Focus Map will help you stay on track with your moderation goals by identifying and connecting with your why. These are the utterly compelling reasons for you to change your drinking habits and maintain a moderate approach to alcohol into your future. The map focusses on improving your whole life holistically, rather than focussing solely on the undesirable behaviour pattern you wish to eradicate. By planning and focussing your attention on multiple experiences and achievements, you bring a fullness and satisfaction to your life. You begin the process of changing your self-image, raising your self-esteem and your confidence in all areas. Moderation mastery is about creating your best life and moving forward positively, which will strengthen your commitment to a healthier life.

Now that you have identified and connected with your values in Chapter 3 you will have a stronger sense of what is motivating and giving you fulfilment and pleasure in your life. This chapter includes a step-by-step guide for creating your own unique

Future Focus Map. This positive action will take you about thirty minutes to an hour to create initially. However, it is a working document that you can add to throughout your moderation journey. You have learned much already and there is plenty more to experience. Stay committed to your goals because there will always be ups and downs with changing your behaviour.

The Future Focus Map

The Future Focus Map will help you to work towards the life you dream of. To do this, it is crucial to reflect on what has helped or hindered you in your efforts at moderating in the past. You can create a life that is so good that you don't want to escape by overdrinking in a destructive way that invalidates your values and places the things you hold dear in jeopardy.

Changing Values

We know that during a lifetime, the values of an individual may often change and this has a great influence in the maturing out of problematic behaviours. Pleasure seeking behaviour, for example, often tends to correspond with adolescence. However, with people marrying and settling down later in life in our current society this can lead to a prolonged adolescence where drinking heavily extends into the late thirties. A lack of responsibilities up until this point means that a person has little compelling reason to slow down on the 'party lifestyle'.

A change in circumstances can come as quite a shock to many people when they approach parenthood, for example. It can take people a little while to navigate this transition into having a dependent in your care and feeling happy about the new situation. As humans, we often do not like change and have a fear of the unknown. These feelings are completely normal and natural as you enter a new stage of your life. People often report moving from pleasure seeking, to a deeper sense of happiness and contentment in the joy and security of having a family or a stable, long-term relationship. The adjustment of your self-concept simply takes a little time to settle in.

The map allows you to see the sequential flow of your life and how you are growing as a person. It serves as a planning technique and helps you stay focussed on the aspects that are important to you now and in the future. It will ensure that you stay connected to the essence of your true self. It will also help you see how you have changed over time which can be enlightening and motivating.

Embrace Change and Build Resilience

To be successful on this journey, it's important to stay open to change and welcome it into your life—even if it feels uncomfortable at first. You may compare your journey to a tree in the wind, with branches that bow but do not break. You are the tree, bending with the ebb and flow of your life, adapting to new phases, building your skills to cope with and flourish, under sometimes challenging circumstances.

This map will act as an important tool in identifying opportunities and potential pitfalls that you need to be aware of. You are the expert from your own experience and creating a rational inventory of this information will help you in your personal growth and eventual transformation. Many people have reported that the construction of this map was a very cathartic and pleasurable experience. Enjoy!

Trisha, 49, Future Focus Map Example

Part A – The Past

1) My past relationship with alcohol was... Often a way to escape. Hedonistic and reckless at times.

2) Key triggers for overdrinking in the past... Anxiety, depression, emotional turmoil, not being understood or supported emotionally, an argument.

3) Potential personal and professional consequences if you had continued to drink in this way... Short-term impact examples... Awful hangovers, tiredness, lack of focus.

Potential long-term consequences...

Job loss, financial problems, relationship issues, degradation of mental health and confidence.

4) In the past my values centred upon... Education, Fun, Friendship, Passion, Humour.

5) Past estimated weekly unit total... 30–40.

Part B – The Present

1) My current relationship with alcohol is... A working progress but generally pretty good and getting better. Around three lapse moments per year and the rest of the time is moderate

2) Current behaviours relating to alcohol...

+ Mindful, thoughtful, considered, intuitive, sociable.

- Attributing a lapse to a personal failure which increases feelings of shame, guilt and regret.

3) Short term benefits of drinking moderately... Self confidence, feeling calm and relaxed, focussed at work and present with family members, good sleep. Long term benefits of drinking moderately... maintaining good relationships with others, achieving ambitions in work and at home, stable mental health.

4) Key triggers for overdrinking... certain people, places or emotion states. Being very emotionally vulnerable or upset, tiredness, stress or excitement.

5) My core values are... Family, Health, Love, Purpose, Spirituality.

6) Current weekly unit total... 14.

Part C – The Future

1) My future relationship with alcohol will be... calm, considered, enjoyable, sociable, in proportion with other aspects of life, a small part of my life.

2) Mastering moderation is crucially important for me because... I'm feeling so much happier and more confident since I cut down, I'm excited about where my life will lead me now, I have the opportunity to shine in all areas. The past is the past and I have learnt so much and now it's time to move on positively. My health is my priority as well as my family. I enjoy looking after myself and others.

3) I will live out my values by... Looking after my family well and enjoying time with them, staying healthy by going to the gym regularly and eating nourishing food, loving my partner; listening and considering their needs, spending quality time together.

4) In the future I want to feel... In tune with my body, grounded, happy and safe. Always having things to look forward to and enjoying a sense of purpose.

5) In the next three years I would like to achieve... Buy a house, expand my business, go camping in France.

6) Experiences I would like to have include... Travelling to America, skiing with my family, go to Harry Potter World, cooking lessons, cultivate a garden of my own, attend a writing retreat, decorate my own house, go snorkelling on a reef with colourful fish and coral.

7) Potential stumbling blocks or triggers that may arise in the future that I have to plan for and continue to be aware of and work on... Working too hard/burning out. Triggers for my continued awareness include, tiredness, over excitement, not eating enough, stress, rejection or emotional vulnerability.

8) Positive behaviours and techniques that will support my moderation goals... Limiting the availability of alcohol, tracking units, planning for events and 'playing it forward' to how I want to feel the day after drinking.

9) My 'Self-Care Toolkit' of actions and activities that will support my moderation goals, include... Positive self-talk, empowering hypnotherapy narratives to inspire confidence, seeking emotional support from others during vulnerable times, being mindful of stress levels, having time out in nature, having a massage, attending a retreat, seeing my therapist regularly, being kind to myself and recognising the progress I have made as opposed to comparing myself to others – I am on my own journey.

10) Aspirational future weekly unit total... 14

11) My moderate drinking situations...

- Out to dinner with my husband when I'm feeling emotionally supported and not overly tired
- With my mum and dad who are both moderate drinkers
- With my in-laws who are also moderate drinkers
- At home in the evening, having a couple of drinks before dinner

CREATE YOUR FUTURE FOCUS MAP

Part A – The Past

1) My past relationship with alcohol was...

2) Key triggers for overdrinking in the past...

3) Potential personal and professional consequences if you had continued to drink in this way...

Short-term impact examples...

Potential long-term consequences...

4) In the past my values centred upon...

5) Past estimated weekly unit total...

Part B – The Present

1) My current relationship with alcohol is...

2) Current behaviours relating to alcohol include...

3) Short term benefits of drinking moderately...

Long term benefits of drinking moderately...

4) Key triggers for overdrinking...

5) My core values are...

6) Current weekly unit total...

Part C – The Future

1) My future relationship with alcohol will be...

2) Mastering moderation is crucially important for me because...

3) I will live out my values by...

4) In the future I want to feel...

5) In the next three years I would like to achieve...

6) Experiences I would like to have include...

7) Potential stumbling blocks or triggers that may arise in the future that I have to plan for and continue to be aware of and work on...

8) Positive behaviours and techniques that will support my moderation goals...

9) My 'Self-Care Toolkit' of actions and activities that will support my moderation goals, include...

10) Aspirational future weekly unit total...

11) My moderate drinking situations...

Your map is divided into three sections: Part A, The Past; Part B, The Present; and Part C The Future. It is useful to know about your past, but more importantly, where you really want to be in the future. As you can see from the map example, it is weighted in its space allocation towards what you will become.

Part A: The Past

Step 1; My past relationship with alcohol was...

Answer this question honestly and from the heart. Often, we begin our drinking careers when we are at an impressionable age and are not aware of the potential pitfalls of overconsumption. We might hear about the danger of drugs and alcohol from adults in an assembly or in a lesson at school, but that may be different from experiencing it in the context of your life. Often, we need to experience things first to grow and develop.

Advertising campaigns, films and television can often glamorise the use of alcohol in social situations. We see alcohol either used to enhance a vibrant occasion or picture someone abusing it with their life at rock bottom, with nothing in between. This may give us a skewed perception of the drug as something to be prized and yet feared in equal quantity.

The reality is that there are many shades of grey in relation to how people use or abuse the substance throughout their life. A great deal of these people mature out of problems with alcohol and you can too. It does not mean that if you have not done this by the time you are 30 years old that you will not be able to do so. If you have the desire to change destructive habits at any age you can do it. Life is a learning curve and the pretence that we should have all aspects of our life perfected by the age of 30 is misleading, as much as it is damaging. Education and personal development are a lifelong process. Many people report that their original relationship with alcohol was one of naivety in their youth, that changed later to an emotional crutch at certain points in their life when they had a demanding job or relationship. It was only at this stage that they started to notice the problematic aspects of alcohol and in turn sought to change their relationship with it.

Step 2; Write down your key triggers for overdrinking in the past...

A trigger can be an emotional state, thoughts, physical states, person(s), place or circumstance that has often led to overdrinking in your past. A good example often reported can be a wedding. What is it about weddings that lead people to overdrink? Many people say that there are many potential triggers, including how it can be an unexpectedly emotional day; a long drinking opportunity; copious amounts of alcohol are freely available; the pressure of expectation to have fun; and seeing family members who you don't get on with. The list can go on!

You will begin to identify times when you are more likely to overdrink and need to make decisions on how to manage such events. Some triggers may no longer exist, such as heavy drinking at university events. However, be aware that if you meet up with old friends there may be that expectation of excess because that is the reference point you have with that particular group of people. It is an interesting exercise and will greatly inform your journey and help you see where you were in life, how it differs from now, and most importantly where you really want to get to.

There are people who shun responsibility and live like a student forever. But most of us want to move on in our lives and achieve corresponding rewards, such as security and a home that we can call our own as opposed to shared living. Ultimately, it is up to you to decide on the journey that your life takes. What makes one person happy and fulfilled is not for anyone else to preside on. These ideas are based on your life experience and your aspirations. Seeing it mapped out is a remarkably effective way to reflect and make appropriate adjustments as new information comes to light.

AMELIA, 32, USED HER SELF-KNOWLEDGE TO IMPROVE HER CHANCES OF SUCCESS

When Amelia, a marketing manager, overconsumed alcohol her behaviour could be destructive within her personal and professional relationships. She remembered times when she had argued fiercely with her partner and on other occasions when she had embarrassed herself at a work social function. Through her reflections about her Future Focus Map and also by collecting data from the Lapse Exercise in her diary, she realised that there was a clear link between feeling stressed in her work life and overdrinking. As a result, Amelia decided that she would not drink alcohol if she was feeling stressed or particularly tired. She also realised that she had the power to shape her life to be more emotionally supportive.

When you apply this method, you build your self-knowledge about situations where you can safely drink and others when it is best avoided, thus strengthening your moderation journey. Alan Marlett argued that one of the most common mistakes of people trying to curb problematic behaviours is focussing on whether they are strong enough to change rather than on specific methods of coping. He helpfully reminded us that, "It is like trying to ride a bike. You make mistakes and learn, and you don't give up if you don't immediately find your balance. If your bicycle is faulty or missing a wheel, then it needs mending, focussing on willing it to work rather than fixing it won't help you to ride."

Deal With the Past

We all have a past, and many people have experienced difficult times. As you can see from the layout, this map is predominantly what we term in therapy circles as 'solution focussed', which means there is not a strong emphasis on reliving aspects of our past.

It is important to note however, if you find out that there are past events which continue to bring you distress in your daily life, it would be sensible to consider talking therapy, such as counselling or psychotherapy. For other people it may be a case of attending to the past through trauma therapy. In time, this may allow you to process your experiences and feel better, so you can be happier and more successful in your improving relationship with alcohol and indeed your life in general.

The Interplay of Psychological Conditions and Alcohol

There is a strong correlation between past trauma, anxiety, depression and other mental health issues and the overuse of alcohol. It is valuable to explore these for yourself before or during your moderation journey to give you the best chance of sustained change. If we try to reduce our alcohol intake without dealing with the underlying causes or risk factors such as problematic levels of anxiety, undertaking a moderation plan can be considered a 'sticking plaster approach', which will only lead to temporary results.

If you consider that you have significant anxiety or depressive symptoms in addition to an alcohol issue for example, it is an excellent idea to seek further advice and treatment for this at the same time or before embarking on this plan.

Step 3; Potential personal and professional consequences if I continued to drink in this way...

Please divide this section into the short-term and long-term impacts.

Short-term impact examples might include: Missing deadlines at work; tension or conflict in personal relationships; elevated anxiety the morning after drinking; and poor sleep.

Potential long-term consequences might include: Loss of a relationship or job; a serious health condition such as cirrhosis of the liver etc.

Step 4; In the past my values centred on...

A value is a belief about something worth striving for. Often people confront and seek to change their behaviours when they are not in line with their values. Life events, such as: starting a business; having a child; or getting married, can all alter what we believe is worth striving for.

ADAM, 57, TUNED INTO HIS DEEPLY-HELD VALUES TO CHANGE HIS BEHAVIOUR

Adam was a successful businessman who recognised that overdrinking, particularly during the working week, was affecting his productivity at work. He identified that a value for him was health and providing financial security for his family, yet he felt that his overdrinking was jeopardising those aspects of his life and making him unhappy. In his youth, drinking with friends after work had been a bigger focus for him and had been how he let off steam after a tough day at the office. More recently, he had seen his sleep and general health suffer.

He carefully reduced his drinking gradually from 80 units a week to 15. He developed new ways of dealing with the pressure of work and used sport as a new way to unwind, as well as being social. Now, he regularly talks about how he does not wish to return to his old ways and has never felt better. His family life and finances are thriving. He considers his overdrinking more as a memory of the past as he tunes in with his deeply-held value of security and health to guide his behaviour in the present and the future. His identity has subtly changed, moving on in his life in a way that makes him feel happy and healthy. He also lost weight naturally which was a great bonus for him!

When our behaviour is in line with our values, we feel good. If it infringes on what we hold dear to our sense of self, it can make us uneasy. It is completely normal to experience a transition in values and corresponding behaviour. Fun and pleasure may well have been a key value earlier in life and it is a natural transition to want other things as we progress in life. For example, the mother in her thirties who would have been a regular on the party circuit sees things differently now she has a baby to protect and nurture. She experiences a shifting of identity as her priorities change. While she may have predominantly sought pleasure in her twenties, now in her later thirties she gains much fulfilment in seeing her baby happy and content, giggling in the highchair. Ten years prior, she would not have given babies a second thought!

Wisdom that we acquire through our life experiences is a great asset in shaping our future achievements and fulfilment. Raising happy and healthy children is an amazing achievement and takes much dedication and hard work. You will understand this if you have children in your life, either your own or maybe you are a godmother or godfather, aunt, or uncle. It is fantastic to be working on your relationship with alcohol so you can be a good role model, taking pride in how you live and look after yourself, so the children in your life too will learn to place a high value on their health and wellbeing in years to come.

Step 5; Past estimated weekly unit total on average...

Part B: The Present

Start in the present and answer honestly in your own words.

Step 1; My current relationship with alcohol is...

There is no right or wrong answer to this question; write your answer from the heart.

Step 2; Current behaviours relating to alcohol...

Firstly, identify positive behaviours, such as ways in which you are handling alcohol well. For example, always eating before having a drink or counting units on a weekly basis. Another example might be, recognising when you are stressed and not drinking. It is important to recognise the skills and behaviours that you already possess and build on your current strengths.

Secondly, identify and note down behaviours that are unhelpful in relation to handling alcohol, such as, continuing to drink in situations that are triggering for you. An example might be continuing to attend high-risk situations, without a moderation plan, such as where intoxication is the general expectation (for example, hen and stag nights).

Another example may be keeping large amounts of alcohol stored in the house because for many people this can lead to regular overdrinking. A bottle of wine shared with your partner with dinner can be a pleasant and moderate experience. However, many people who have ample supplies in the home are tempted to have a couple of extra glasses late into the evening. In this way, limiting the supply and the time in which you allow yourself to drink can be a simple, yet powerful tool.

Step 3; Short-term benefits of drinking moderately and long-term benefits of drinking moderately...

An example of short-term benefits of drinking moderately might include: brighter skin; less headaches; more energy; improved sleep; feeling calmer; more harmonious relationship with your partner; being a more reliable parent; and increased focus at work.

Long-term benefits of drinking moderately might include: better mental and physical health; progression and satisfaction at work; successful and happy relationships with others; improved self-image and confidence; and easier to maintain a healthy weight.

Step 4; Identify your key triggers for overdrinking...

Examples of triggers can be perfectionist thinking and certain people, places or emotion states?

Step 5; My values are...

Record your core values, your beliefs about things worth striving for in your life currently. You will have completed this activity in Chapter 3. Examples might include: health; family; love; and education.

Step 6; Current weekly unit total on average...

Record here...

Part C: The Future

Now, for the most exciting section! Here, you think of how you really want your life to be as you visualise and embrace change. It is time to move towards the person you really want to become.

Step 1; My future relationship with alcohol will be...

Here is your chance to decide what kind of drinker you want to be. It might be useful to consider the definition of a moderate drinker as discussed in Chapter 2. In summary, it is someone who enjoys the relaxing and social benefits of an occasional drink or two, but without the negative consequences. Drinking is in proportion with the rest of your life. An example might include a small enjoyable aspect of my life.

Step 2; Mastering moderation is crucially important for me because...

An example might include, to be happy, healthy and ensure that I have a good life and can achieve my potential in personal and professional spheres.

Step 3; I will live out my values by...

These are the continued actions you will take in your daily life that support your values. If one of your core values is family, then it might be that it is important to you to always be reliable so your family can depend on you. Actions you can take in relation to this might be to avoid high-risk potential drinking situations, which you may have attended in the past. Another example might be the value of your health, where the action could be meal planning and shopping online at the supermarket to ensure you are well stocked with healthy food to prepare your planned meals. Security is another value that is important to many people, so making good decisions around money such as sticking to a weekly budget may be an action that can help you live out your core belief.

Step 4; In the future I want to feel...

Many people who master moderation report feeling healthier, happier, fitter, slimmer, calmer, more confident and in control of their lives in comparison to when they overdrank. Write down all the positive feelings and emotions you want to bring into your life.

Step 5; In the next three years I want to achieve...

Add the milestones you want to achieve such as: gain a qualification; change career; buy a house; have another child; set up a business; or move abroad. The sky is the limit. Think carefully and design the home and life that you really want for yourself and those people you hold dear.

Step 6; Experiences I want to have include...

This answer may include something you have done in the past that you have enjoyed, such as scuba diving, or gardening. Or, they can be something you have never tried before, such as a bungee jump, or skydive. It may include places you wish to travel and it will become a reality when the time is right.

Step 7; Potential stumbling blocks and triggers that may arise in the future, which you have to plan for and continue to be aware of and work on...

Look ahead and make estimations about events, people, places or emotional states that will challenge you in the future. Examples might include: a house move; having a baby; and attending a wedding, birthday, or anniversary party. These events may be a one-off situation or cover a longer period, such as a holiday or moving house. Think about how you can navigate these situations so they do not cause you to overdrink. What strategies can you put in place to support your goals? You can use the work you completed in Chapter 4 for more inspiration relating to your triggers.

Step 8; List positive behaviours and techniques that will support your moderation goals...

These are positive techniques or behaviours that you have learnt about in this book and through your experience of moderating so far, which you think will help you in the future. Examples might include: setting limits around how much you might drink on a given occasion; or avoiding drinking in certain situations that you know may be risky for you.

Step 9; Write down your 'Self-Care Toolkit'...

Your 'Self-Care Toolkit' is a collection of strategies or activities that you have personally found through reading, research and your wider life experience to be helpful in maintaining your physical and mental wellbeing to support your moderation journey. Examples might include: exercising three times a week; meditation for ten minutes a day; eating healthily; having a few special bath nights a week; tennis; or a long bike ride at the weekend.

Step 10; Aspirational future weekly unit total on average...
This will potentially be somewhere around the 14 unit mark on average.

Step 11; My moderate drinking situations...
These are times when you feel you can safely moderate your alcohol intake.

Your Way Forward

Well done on your progress so far. Your Future Focus Map is a working document that you can come back to and add further detail to, as you progress on your moderation journey. When you have a clear grasp of where you are moving to in life and what is really important for your health and happiness, it is so much easier not to get derailed. You are developing an undercurrent of strength that stops you becoming snagged on small branches at the side of the river because you now have a forward movement and sense of purpose flowing through your life. It is critically important on this journey to feel good about yourself and to know where you are going with a clear destination. This helps build your resilience and core sense of self. It can make you feel good to write things down and seeing them in front of you makes them real and tangible. It is also important to remember that being a moderator is something that takes practice, patience and refinement, as you tap into your limitless potential for positive growth.

Please go to the webpage www.drinklesslivewell.com to access the hypnosis recording that compliments this chapter entitled; *Positive Future Focus.*

I wish you all the very best on your journey.

Chapter by Chapter Quotation References

Chapter 1
Tuli Kupferberg; American author (1923–2010)

Chapter 2
Sanhita Baruah; Indian author

Chapter 3
Marilyn Ferguson; American author (1938–2008)

Chapter 4
Socrates; Greek philosopher (470 BC–399 BC)

Chapter 5
Dalai Lama; Buddhist spiritual leader

Chapter 6
Otto Rank; Austrian psychoanalyst, writer and philosopher (1884–1939)

Chapter 7
Tansy Forrest; Hypnotherapist

Chapter 8
Audre Lorde; American writer, radical feminist, professor (1934–1992)

Chapter 9
Dr. John David Sinclair; American scientist and researcher. He discovered the Alcohol Deprivation Effect (ADE) and targeted a pharmacological extinction approach for the medication-assisted treatment for Alcohol Use Disorder (AUD), known as The Sinclair Method (TSM) (1943 – 2015)

Chapter 10
Kevin W Pearson; American CEO and Elder in the Church of Jesus Christ of Latter-Day Saints

Contact the Author

If this book has helped you and you want to contact the author, please go to any of the following platforms.

Youtube
www.youtube.com/@tansyforrest

Instagram
www.instagram.com/tansy_forrest

Book Website
www.drinklesslivewell.com

Personal Website
www.tansyforrest.com

References, Recommended Readings and Resources

Chapter 2

1. Alcohol In England, 2022. *Alcohol Toolkit Study,* National Institute for Health Research, viewed 4 June 2022, <https://www.alcoholinengland.info/graphs/monthly-tracking-kpi>.

2. Wikipedia, 2023. *History of Alcoholics Anonymous,* Wikipedia, viewed 19 March 2021, <https://en.wikipedia.org/wiki/History_of_Alcoholics_Anonymous>.

3. Alcoholics Anonymous (2020) *Interesting Statistics,* Alcoholic Anonymous, viewed 21 March 2021,<https://www.alcoholics-anonymous.org.uk/professionals/interesting-statistics>.

4. National Institute on Drug Abuse, 2018. *The Science of Drug Use and Addiction: The Basics,* National Institute on Drug Abuse, viewed 21 March 2021, < https://archives.drugabuse.gov/publications/media-guide/science-drug-use-addiction-basics#:~:text=Addiction%20is%20defined%20as%20a,disorder%20and%20a%20mental%20illness.>.

5. Substance Abuse and Mental Health Services Administration; Office of the Surgeon General (US). 2016. *Facing Addiction in America: The Surgeon General's Report on Alcohol, Drugs, and Health.* [Online]. Washington: US Department of Health and Human Services. [Accessed 25 March 2021]. Available from: https://pubmed.ncbi.nlm.nih.gov/28252892/.

6. Turner, C. 2020. *The Clinician's Guide to Alcohol Moderation: Alternative Methods and Management Techniques.* New York: Routledge.

7. *The Business of Recovery.* 2015. [Online]. Directed by Adam Finberg. America: Greg Horvath Productions. Available from Amazon Prime. [Viewed 28 March 2021].

8. The American Psychiatric Association. 2013. *Diagnostic and Statistical Manual of Mental Disorders.* 5th edn. Washington: American Psychiatric Association.

9. Office for National Statistics, 2022. *Overview of the UK Population: 2020,* Office for National Statistics, viewed 26 March 2021, < https://www.ons.gov.uk/peoplepopulationandcommunity/populationandmigration/populationestimates/articles/overviewoftheukpopulation/2020>.

10. The Department of Health. 2016. *UK Chief Medical Officers' Alcohol Guidelines Review: Summary of the Proposed New Guidelines.* [Online]. London: The Department of Health. [Date accessed 27 March 2021]. Available from: https://assets.publishing.service.gov.uk/government/uploads/system/uploads/attachment_data/file/489795/summary.pdf# .

11. Centers for Disease Control and Prevention, 2022. *Dietary Guidelines for Alcohol,* Centers for Disease Control and Prevention, viewed 28 March 2021,< https://www.cdc.gov/alcohol/fact-sheets/moderate-drinking.htm>.

12. Sobell, M. B. and Sobell, L.C. 1995. *Controlled Drinking After Twenty-Five Years: How Important was the Great Debate? The Journal of Addiction,* vol. 90, no. 9, pp. 1149-1153. Available at: https://pubmed.ncbi.nlm.nih.gov/7580815/ (Accessed: 29 March 2021).

13. Hasin, D. S. and Grant, B. F. 2015. *The National Epidemiologic Survey on Alcohol and Related Conditions (NESARC) Waves 1 and 2: Review and Summary of Findings. The Journal of Social Psychiatry and Psychiatric Epidemiology,* vol. 50, no. 11, pp.1609-1640. Available at: https://www.ncbi.nlm.nih.gov/pmc/articles/PMC4618096/ (Accessed: 29 March 2021).

14. Babor, T.F. et al. 1996. *World Health Organisation Brief Intervention Study Group: A Cross-National Trial of Brief Interventions with Heavy Drinkers. The American Journal of Public Health,* vol. 86, no. 7, pp.948-955. Available at: https://ajph.aphapublications.org/doi/pdf/10.2105/AJPH.86.7.948 (Accessed: 1 April 2021).

15. The Department of Health. 2008. *The Birmingham Untreated Heavy Drinkers Project: Final Report.* [Online]. Birmingham: Birmingham University. [Date accessed 15th April 2021]. Available from: https://assets.publishing.service.gov.uk/government/uploads/system/uploads/attachment_data/file/215795/dh_123886.pdf .

16. Cahalan, D. and Room, R. 1987. *Drinking Patterns and Drinking Problems in 1984: Results from a General Population Survey. The Journal for Alcoholism: Clinical and Experimental Research,* vol. 11, no.2, pp.167-75. Available at: https://pubmed.ncbi.nlm.nih.gov/3296836/ (Accessed: 3 April 2021).

17. Peele, S. 1991. *The Truth About Addiction and Recovery.* New York: Simon and Schuster.

18. The World Health Organisation. 1977. *Alcohol Related Disabilities.* Geneva: World Health Organisation.

19. Turner, C. 2020. *The Clinician's Guide to Alcohol Moderation: Alternative Methods and Management Techniques.* New York: Routledge.

20. Hitchens, C. 2003. *Living Proof,* Vanity Fair, viewed 17 March 2021, < https://www.vanityfair.com/news/2003/03/hitchens-200303>.

Chapter 3

1. Peele, S. 1991. *The Truth About Addiction and Recovery.* New York: Simon and Schuster.

2. Covey, S. 1989. *The Seven Habits of Highly Effective People.* New York:

Simon and Schuster.

3. Frankl, V. 2004. *Man's Search for Meaning: The Classic Tribute to Hope from the Holocaust.* London: Random House.

Chapter 4

1. Rotgers, F. 2002. *Responsible Drinking: A Moderation Management Approach for Problem Drinkers.* CA: New Harbinger Publications.

2. Peele, S. 1991. *The Truth About Addiction and Recovery.* New York: Simon and Schuster.

3. The Global Drugs Survey. 2020. *GDS Covid-19 Special Edition: Key Findings Report* [Online]. 10th Edition. London: Global Drugs Survey. [Date accessed 1 April 2021]. Available from : https://www.globaldrugsurvey.com/gds-covid-19-special-edition-key-findings-report/ .

4. Drinkaware, (n.d), *Alcohol and Mental Health,* Viewed 2 April 2021, Drinkaware < https://www.drinkaware.co.uk/facts/health-effects-of-alcohol/mental-health/alcohol-and-mental-health >.

5. Turner, C. 2020. *The Clinician's Guide to Alcohol Moderation: Alternative Methods and Management Techniques.* New York: Routledge.

6. Drinkaware, (n.d), *Alcohol and Mental Health,* Viewed 2 April 2021, < https://www.drinkaware.co.uk/facts/health-effects-of-alcohol/mental-health/alcohol-and-mental-health >.

Chapter 5

1. Rotgers, F. 2002. *Responsible Drinking: A Moderation Management Approach for Problem Drinkers.* CA: New Harbinger Publications.

2. Drinkaware 2022. *UK Low Risk Drinking Guidelines,* Viewed 2 April 2021, Drinkaware, < https://www.drinkaware.co.uk/facts/alcoholic-drinks-and-units/low-risk-drinking-guidelines >.

3. Centers for Disease Control and Prevention, 2022. *Dietary Guidelines for Alcohol,* Centers for Disease Control and Prevention, viewed 28 March 2021,< https://www.cdc.gov/alcohol/fact-sheets/moderate-drinking.htm>.

4. Rotgers, F. 2002 *Responsible Drinking: A Moderation Management Approach for Problem Drinkers.* CA: New Harbinger Publications.

5. Griffin, K. , 2010, *Interview with G. Alan Marlatt: Surfing The Urge,* Viewed 3rd April 2021, Inquiring Mind, < https://www.inquiringmind.com/article/2602_w_marlatt-interview-with-g-alan-marlatt-surfing-the-urge/ >.

Chapter 6

1. Tucker, J. and Marlatt, G. 2001. *Changing Addictive Behaviour: Bridging Clinical and Public Health Strategies.* New York: Guilford.

2. Drinkaware 2021. *Dr Sarah Jarvis Discusses How to Stop Drinking Completely.* 7th September. Available at: https://www.youtube.

com/watch?v=6EVJ4gQEXXo
(Accessed: September 2021).

3. Rotgers, F. 2002. *Responsible Drinking: A Moderation Management Approach for Problem Drinkers.* CA: New Harbinger Publications.

4. Turner, C. 2020. *The Clinician's Guide to Alcohol Moderation: Alternative Methods and Management Techniques.* New York: Routledge.

5. Griffin, K. 2010. *Interview with G. Alan Marlatt: Surfing The Urge,* Viewed 3rd April 2021, Inquiring Mind, < https://www.inquiringmind.com/article/2602_w_marlatt-interview-with-g-alan-marlatt-surfing-the-urge/ >.

6. Rotgers, F. 2002. *Responsible Drinking: A Moderation Management Approach for Problem Drinkers.* CA: New Harbinger Publications.

7. Economy, P. 2018. *This is the Way You Need to Write Down Your Goals for Faster Success,* Inc.com, Viewed 15th September 2021, <https://www.inc.com/peter-economy/this-is-way-you-need-to-write-down-your-goals-for-faster-success.html#:~:text=Psychology%20professor%20Dr.,if%20you%20write%20them%20down>.

Chapter 7

1. Marlatt, G.A. and Donovan, D.M. 2005. *Relapse Prevention: Maintenance Strategies in the Treatment of Addictive Behaviours* (2nd edition). New York: Guilford Press.

Chapter 8

1. Sarah's Self Care Corner, 2023. *Introduction to Self-Care,* Sarah's Self Care Corner, Viewed 17 September 2021, < https://sites.psu.edu/shkrcl1/2022/01/26/introduction-to-self-care/ >.

2. Rotgers, F. 2002. *Responsible Drinking: A Moderation Management Approach for Problem Drinkers.* CA: New Harbinger Publications.

3. Larimer, M.E., Palmer R.S, and Marlatt, G.A. 1999. *Relapse Prevention: An Overview of Marlatt's Cognitive-behavioural Model. The Journal for Alcohol Research and Health,* vol. 23, no. 2, pp. 151-60. Available at: https://pubmed.ncbi.nlm.nih.gov/10890810/ (Accessed: 20 September 2021).

4. Lawton, G. 2020. *This Book Could Save Your Life.* London: John Murray.

5. Miller, W. 2013. *Controlling Your Drinking: Tools to Make Moderation Work for You* (2nd edition). New York: Guilford.

6. Li, J., Vitiello, M.V. and Gooneratne, N.S. 2018. *Sleep in Normal Aging. The Journal for Clinical Sleep Medicine,* vol. 13, no. 1 , pp.1-11. Available at: https://www.ncbi.nlm.nih.gov/pmc/articles/PMC5841578/ (Accessed: 25 September 2021).

7. Hölzel, B. et al. 2011 *Mindfulness Practice Leads to Increases in Regional Brain Gray Matter Density. Psychiatry Research,* vol. 191, no. 1, pp.36-43. Available at: https://www.

ncbi.nlm.nih.gov/pmc/articles/
PMC3004979/ (Accessed: 27
September 2021).

8. Stahl, B. and Goldstein, E.
2010. *A Mindfulness- Based Stress
Reduction Workbook.* Oakland: New
Harbinger.

9. Lawton, G. 2020. *This Book Could
Save Your Life.* London: John
Murray.

10. Patel, A. et al. 2011. *General
Practitioners' Views and Experiences
of Counselling for Physical Activity
Through the New Zealand Green
Prescription Program. BMC Journal
of Family Practice,* vol. 12, no. 119,
pp.119-127. Available at: https://
bmcprimcare.biomedcentral.
com/articles/10.1186/1471-2296-
12-119#citeas (Accessed: 27
September 2021).

11. The Forest Bathing Institute, 2023.
*New Research Compares Forrest
Bathing and Mindfulness,* The
Forest Bathing Institute, viewed
November 15 2021, < https://tfb.
institute/scientific-research/>.

12. Morris, J. and Crawford, M.
1958. *Coronary Heart Disease and
Physical Activity of Work. British
Medical Journal,* vol. 2, no. 5111, pp.
1485-96. Available at: https://www.
ncbi.nlm.nih.gov/pmc/articles/
PMC2027542/ (Accessed: 28
September 2021).

13. Rotgers, F. 2002. *Responsible
Drinking: A Moderation
Management Approach for Problem
Drinkers.* CA: New Harbinger
Publications.

14. Perreault, K. et al 2017. *Does
Physical Activity Moderate the
Association Between Alcohol
Drinking and All Cause Cancer
and Cardiovascular Diseases
Mortality? A Pooled Analysis of
Eight British Population Cohorts.
British Journal of Sports Medicine,*
vol. 51, no. 8, pp. 651-7. Available
at: https://pubmed.ncbi.nlm.nih.
gov/27581162/ (Accessed: 5 October
2021).

Chapter 9

1. Anderson, K. 2010. *How to Change
Your Drinking: A Harm Reduction
Guide to Alcohol.* New York: The
HAMS Harm Reduction Network.

2. Turner, C. 2020. *The Clinician's
Guide to Alcohol Moderation:
Alternative Methods and
Management Techniques.* London:
Routledge.

3. Eskapa, R. 2012. *The Cure For
Alcoholism: The Medically Proven
Way to Eliminate Alcohol Addiction.*
Dallas: BenBella Books.

4. Addiction Treatment Forum,
2002. *Evidence for the Efficacy of
Naltrexone in the Treatment of
Alcohol Dependence, Substance
Abuse and Mental Health Services
Administration,* viewed November
11 2023, < https://www.samhsa.
gov/sites/default/files/programs_
campaigns/medication_assisted/
efficacy-naltrexone-treatment-
alcohol-dependence.pdf >.

5. *One Little Pill.* 2014. [Online].
Directed by Adam Schomer.

America: Zard Productions. Available from Amazon Prime. [Viewed on 28 March 2023].

6. C Three Foundation, 2023. viewed 26 March 2023, < https://cthreefoundation.org/>.

7. Ted x Talks (2016) *How I overcame alcoholism* Available at: https://www.youtube.com/watch?v=6EghiY_s2ts&t=221s, Accessed: 23rd December 2023.

8. Sinclair, D. 2001. *Evidence About the use of Naltrexone and for Different Ways of Using it in the Treatment of Alcoholism.* Journal of Alcohol and Alcoholism, vol. 36,no.1, pp2-10. Available at https://academic.oup.com/alcalc/article/36/1/2/137995 (Accessed: 5 October 2023).

9. National Institute of Health Care Excellence, 2014. *Alcohol-use disorders: diagnosis, assessment and management of harmful drinking (high-risk drinking) and alcohol dependence,* viewed November 11 2023, <https://www.nice.org.uk/guidance/cg115/chapter/Recommendations>.

10. NHS, 2022. *Treatment, Alcohol Misuse,* viewed November 11 2023, < https://www.nhs.uk/conditions/alcohol-misuse/treatment/> .

11. National Library of Medicine, 2015. *Naltrexone and Liver Disease,* viewed November 11th 2023 < https://www.ncbi.nlm.nih.gov/pmc/articles/PMC4657311/ >.

12. Drugs.com, 2024. *What to avoid when taking naltrexone?* viewed May 6 2025, < https://www.drugs.com/medical-answers/avoid-taking-naltrexone-3548600/>.

13. NHS, Royal Free Hospital, 2025. *Nalmefene,* viewed May 5 2025, < https://www.royalfree.nhs.uk/patients-and-visitors/patient-information-leaflets/nalmefene#what-medicines-should-i-avoid-with-nalmefene-selincro>.

14. Sinclair, D. 2001. *Evidence About the use of Naltrexone and for Different Ways of Using it in the Treatment of Alcoholism. Journal of Alcohol and Alcoholism,* vol. 36, no.1, pp2-10. Available at https://academic.oup.com/alcalc/article/36/1/2/137995 (Accessed: 5 October 2023).

Chapter 10

1. Percy-Smith, B. 2011. *Understanding and Supporting Young People Who are NEET: Implications for Service Development.* Bristol: University of the West of England.

Printed in Dunstable, United Kingdom

74088499R00127